eve & mary

A SIMPLY BIBLE STUDY

CARMEN BEASLEY

For God's daughters.

SO GOD CREATED MAN
IN HIS OWN IMAGE,
IN THE IMAGE OF GOD
HE CREATED HIM;
MALE AND FEMALE
HE CREATED THEM.

GENESIS 1:27

table of *contents*

EVE & MARY | A **SIMPLY BIBLE** STUDY

INTRODUCTION

STUDY CONTENT
PART I

PART II

APPENDIX

"THIS AT LAST IS
BONE OF MY BONES.
AND FLESH OF MY FLESH;
SHE SHALL BE CALLED WOMAN,
BECAUSE SHE WAS
TAKEN OUT OF MAN.

GENESIS 2:23

welcome

KNOWING GOD
THROUGH TWO WOMEN
OF THE BIBLE

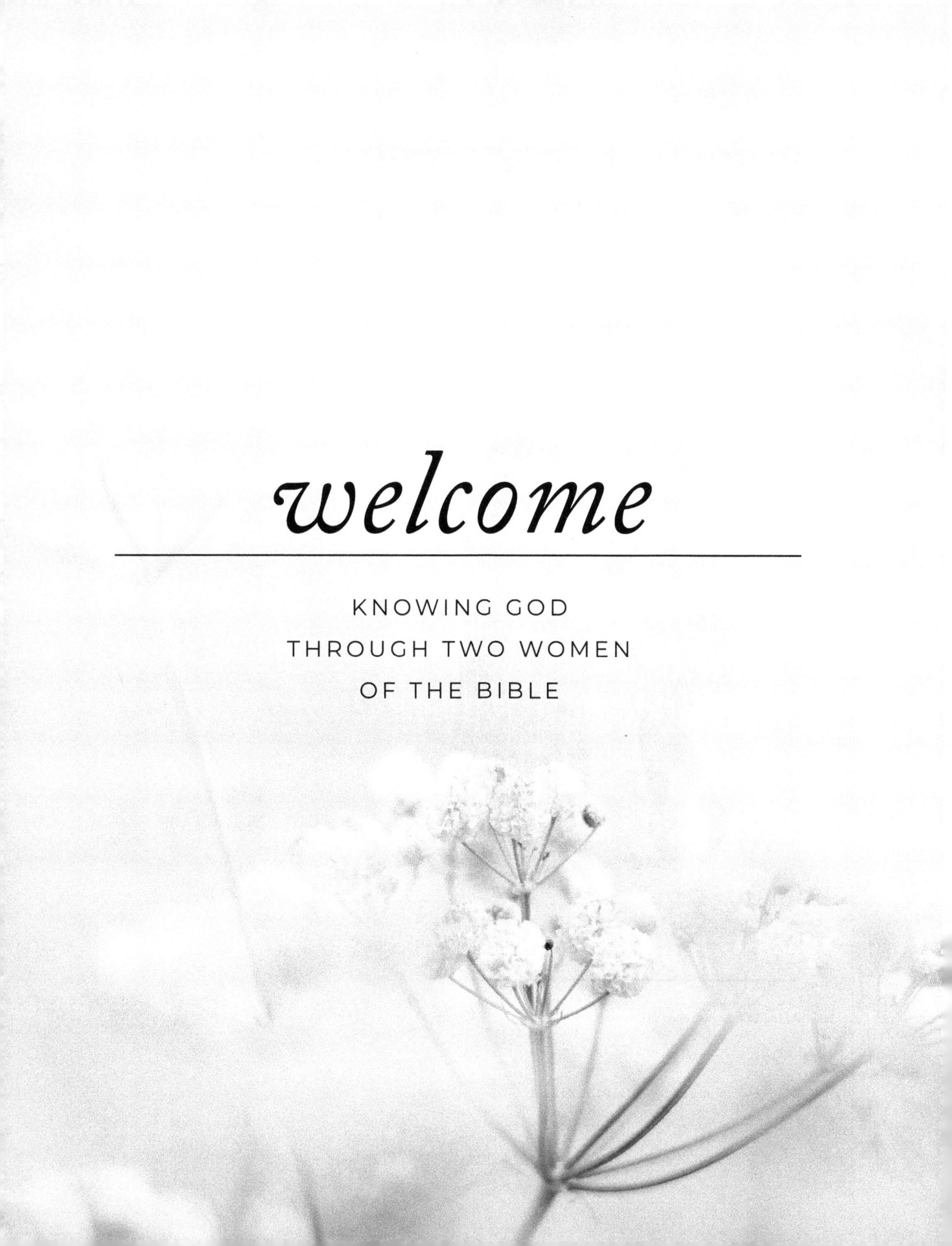

welcome to *eve & mary*

THE INSPIRATION BEHIND THE STUDY

The following piece of art inspired this study:

Mary & Eve by Scott Erickson

Scott Erickson based his artwork on this piece, which has also served as inspiration:

My mother, my daughter,
Life-giving Eve,
Do not be ashamed, do
not grieve,
The former things have
passed away,
Our God has brought us
to a New Day.
See, I am with Child.
Through whom all will
be reconciled.
O Eve! My sister, my
friend,
We will rejoice together
Forever
Life without end.

By Sister Columba
Guare

Mary & Eve by Sister Grace Remington

welcome to *eve & mary*

KNOWING GOD THROUGH TWO WOMEN OF THE BIBLE

Hi friend,

I am excited to offer this study of Eve and Mary so that we might better know and enjoy God Himself. These two remarkable women of the Bible have more in common than meets the eye. Together, they lay the foundation for the good news, the gospel of Jesus Christ. Without them, the good news of Jesus would not exist as we know it. Our goal is not just to learn from Eve and Mary but to know Jesus and enjoy Him.

Inspired by artwork depicting Eve and Mary together, I have contemplated these two biblical heroines for some time. Perhaps referring to them as heroines will raise eyebrows. After all, their struggles differ greatly from those of Moses or David. Still, I invite you to examine Scripture closely for yourself. While God remains the true Hero of the Bible, He often reveals His glory and accomplishes His works through human beings, including Eve and Mary. Readers today can learn more about God through the lives of these life-giving women.

THOSE OF US IN THE CHURCH OFTEN REVERE MARY. Although not all Christian traditions recognize her as a canonized saint, all Christians celebrate her once a year during Advent and Christmas. She will always be remembered and honored as the mother of Jesus.

BUT EVE? A HEROINE? ISN'T THE WORLD A MESS BECAUSE OF HER?

Eve is often remembered as an instigator of sin. We must grasp the grave significance of her and Adam's disobedience. Understanding humanity's sin problem is crucial to making sense of the Bible and our lives. Their sin shattered our glorious resemblance of and relationship to a glorious God. Moreover, we cannot truly comprehend God's grace without first recognizing the devastating consequences of Adam's sin, Eve's sin, and our own sin: death.

Yet, I wonder if we have overlooked Eve's glory in our finger-pointing haste.

Consider this: when you think of Eve, do you remember her for her God-given glory and her place as the mother of all the living? Or do you quickly focus on her sin? Could it be possible that we, along with much of church history, have been unkind to Eve? Could an unmerciful view of Eve have led to a domino effect of unkindness towards others, particularly women, since the very beginning?

In his book, *The Scarlet Letter,* published in 1850, American author Nathaniel Hawthorne explores themes of sin and guilt. Set in a legalistic Puritan colony, the main character, Hester Prynne, conceives a daughter with a man she is not married to. As punishment, she is forced to wear a scarlet letter A, an outward reminder of her sin of adultery. Her entire community shuns her. She lives and raises her daughter alone outside the village, making a living through her beautiful needlework. Forever alone and marked by the scarlet letter, she remains mindful and compassionate towards others, helping the poor and the sick. Throughout the book, questions linger for the reader: Is a sinner forever condemned, or is she forgivable, redeemable? Hawthorne's novel highlights the ugly human propensity to finger-point and remain unforgiving towards others and even oneself.

Many throughout the ages have believed that God treats us similarly: we are cast out of His village without hope for grace and without a second (or a hundredth) chance to receive His forgiveness and love.

So how does God view a "sinner" like Hester, like Eve, or like me? Does God withhold grace and mercy until we clean ourselves up? Jesus refutes this perspective in Matthew 9:13 when he states,

I came not to call the righteous,
but sinners.

MATTHEW 9:13

JESUS CAME TO SAVE US WHILE WE WERE YET SINNERS, BEARERS OF SCARLET LETTERS.

Throughout church history, Eve has certainly worn her own scarlet letter. Yet, a closer look at Genesis also reveals God's gracious, redemptive work through Eve, making her "the mother of all the living." Would Eve not have looked forward in hope to the One who would crush the serpent's head?

This living hope passed from generation to generation from Eve all the way to Mary in the New Testament.

Mary understood that same hope. She looked forward to God's promise. Mary, too, essentially became the mother of all the living. Eve's role as a mother was not easy, nor was Mary's. Mary surely felt the heartache of receiving finger-pointing and judgment from her contemporaries. Carrying Jesus in her womb was akin to wearing a scarlet letter. She undoubtedly faced the brunt of accusations, insidious whispers, and not-so-quiet scorn for being a sinner of the worst kind. After all, who could imagine a *virgin* birth?

Even today, Mary's pregnancy evokes both ridicule and disbelief. Although a virgin birth remains incomprehensible to our logical minds, believers in Jesus trust in God's word and in His almighty power. If Jesus the Messiah were to be born into human flesh and blood, He could only be conceived in such a miraculous way. Furthermore, because Mary remained willing and steadfast amid the pain and suffering of bearing the Son of God, witnessing His death on a cross, and then experiencing the joy of His resurrection, she is beloved as the first disciple of our Lord and Savior—her son, God's Son—Jesus.

Much can be learned from Mary, and much can be learned about God through Mary. However, I also wonder if there isn't much to learn from Eve. Over the years, I, too, have pointed accusing fingers at the first woman, as if she were the very picture of evil. I have found myself cursing her for various pains related to menstrual cycles, childbirth, child-rearing, and even marital tension. More than once, I have declared, "Eve's fault!" or "Thanks for nothing, Eve!" If we're honest, we've all likely pinned an infamous and enduring scarlet letter on her, as if we ourselves are sinless. But in so doing, we fail to remember that Eve was formed by the hand of God, fashioned in His very own image, and received God's very life-breath.

SO, SHOULD WE REMEMBER EVE ONLY FOR HER TRANSGRESSION? More importantly, how does God view Eve? How does *He* respond to her sin? And by the way, isn't Jesus also Eve's offspring?

I am curious and have many more questions. I hope you do, too. All these questions and ideas influence how we envision God's perception of us and His response to our sins.

Curiosity is essential for knowing God through the Bible. In his book *Unspoken Sermons*, George MacDonald—a pastor, scholar, and author who inspired writers like C.S. Lewis and J.R.R. Tolkien—categorizes followers of Jesus into two groups. He refers to the first type of disciple as "dull." In MacDonald's words, the dull follower fails to ask God questions about His Word, either because he is disinterested or believes he already knows all there is to know about God. In contrast, the other type of disciple is eager. An eager disciple approaches God with curiosity, seeking to know Him and to ask Him questions. George MacDonald says, "Questions imply answers. God has put the questions in my heart; He holds the answers in His. I will seek them from Him… I will seek until I find." [1]

---

[1] George MacDonald, **Unspoken Sermons**, 2016, page 24.

Our questions and God's answers hold the utmost importance. They are crucial to our relationship with God and with one another. In this context, our beliefs about Eve significantly influence how we perceive God, ourselves, and others. Our evaluation of Eve affects our ability to accept God's forgiveness for our own sins and our capacity to forgive others as well.

In regard to our own scarlet letters, can we fully accept that Jesus covers our unspeakable sins? Is there any hope for our marred images? Will we forever bear our scarlet letters, or can we trust God to forgive us and clothe us in new garments?

I fully admit that my view of Eve has often smacked of pride. I have even declared out loud, "Praise God that it was Eve and not me! Thank goodness the Bible doesn't say, 'Carmen looked, took, and ate the forbidden fruit!'"

Oh, I confess my pride! See how closely that resembles the Pharisee in Jesus's parable:

> The Pharisee, standing by himself, prayed thus: 'God, I thank you that I am not like other men, extortioners, unjust, adulterers, or even like this tax collector.'
>
> LUKE 18:11

Compare this prayer with the tax collector's prayer in the same parable—a sinner who wore his own scarlet letter before the Jews of his day:

> But the tax collector, standing far off,
> would not even lift up his eyes to heaven,
> but beat his breast, saying, 'God, be
> merciful to me, a sinner!'
>
> LUKE 18:13

Which man does Jesus point to as justified by God and the recipient of His mercy? Is it the one who attends church, fasts twice weekly, and gives tithes, or is it the one who humbles himself, admits he is a sinner, and declares his need for God's mercy? Jesus considers the tax collector justified:

> I tell you, this man went down to his house
> justified, rather than the other. For
> everyone who exalts himself will be
> humbled, but the one who humbles
> himself will be exalted.
>
> LUKE 18:14

Friend, let us humble ourselves as we approach God and search His Word. As we see Eve's need, may we recognize our own. We are all sinners in need of God's mercy and grace. While there are consequences for sin, God offers second chances and more; His grace abounds, connecting us to Mary and God's gift of love that she willingly bore. As we compare and contrast these two women, let us not assume we have all the answers; instead, let us allow God to search our hearts. Let us release our assumptions and presuppositions, particularly everything we might believe we know about God. Let us slow down, be curious, ask questions, and look closely with fresh eyes to comprehend His mercy and love.

LET US MEANDER INSIDE AND OUTSIDE THE GARDEN OF EDEN. Let us see God through Eve's eyes, and Eve through God's eyes.

LET US KNEEL BY THE MANGER AND AT THE FOOT OF THE CROSS WITH MARY. Let us see God through her eyes, and Mary through God's.

LET US REFLECT ON GOD AND ALL THAT HE HAS DONE. In this way, perhaps our study of God and His relationship with these two women, who are the mothers of all the living, will become a life-giving experience, perhaps even a scarlet-letter-abolishing experience through Jesus, the ultimate Life-Giver.

And perhaps, as we do, the tides of church history will change as we learn to extend His grace.

Lord God, thank You for Your heart of compassion and grace demonstrated through Jesus. May we, as men and women saved by Your scarlet-letter-abolishing grace alone, fully receive and believe, and in turn, be quick to extend grace to our brothers and sisters. As we study, unite our hearts and minds with the heart and mind of Jesus.

Friend, thank you for joining this **SIMPLY BIBLE** Eve and Mary study. May you find God's grace on every page. All glory and honor be unto Him.

With joy,

Carmen

PS-For more Bible study tips, please visit and join our online community at **www.simplybiblestudy.org.**

inductive study

AN INTRODUCTION TO **SIMPLY BIBLE**

inductive bible study

AN INTRODUCTION TO **SIMPLY BIBLE**

AS A LITTLE GIRL, I ADORED COLORING BOOKS. Smooth, crisp white pages displayed bold black lines of perfectly drawn figures and characters. The spaces patiently awaited color. Fondly, I remember the joy of opening a new pack of crayons. The waxy smell and the neat little rows of pointed tips colorfully peeked out and tantalized me as if to say, "Try to choose just one!" Creativity awaited. Or so I thought.

When my four children were small, a friend of a friend encouraged me to forgo purchasing coloring books for them. My initial reaction was one of horror, "What? Coloring books are fun! That would be forgoing fun! Plain paper? How boring!" Okay, granted my reaction was a little melodramatic, but I do remember thinking these thoughts.

Instead, this friend insisted that providing children with blank sheets of paper was the way to spur creativity. I could see the wisdom, not to mention, a ream of paper was way cheaper than four new coloring books. And so, I gave it a try. Does this mean I never gave my children coloring books? No! My children certainly enjoyed a few here and there. However, I admit that these books never seemed to offer my children the same kind of joy as coloring books had offered me. And so for the most part, my children simply grew up with lots of plain white paper and a variety of colorful pencils, crayons, and markers.

PLAIN, WHITE PAPER IT WAS. What happened? My kids learned to draw. Not just little stick figures in the middle of the page, but they learned to tell a story using a piece of paper. Masterpieces (or so this mom deems them).

Now, I'm sure no one ever saved one of my coloring book pages. Oh, for sure one sometimes landed on Grandma's refrigerator. However, right now, down in my basement, there remain binders of pictures that my budding artists created over twenty years ago. Why? These pictures were windows into their little souls and minds. For example, if God was not present in a Bible story, my son would draw a big eye in the sky in his depiction of the story. In his little five-year-old heart, he understood that God could see him. Had I handed my children coloring book pages where they filled in the blanks, I would never have had this window into their hearts and minds.

Their works of art tell stories. And I treasure them in my heart.

THIS IS THE GIST OF **SIMPLY BIBLE.** These guides provide a "blank page" for reading and directly engaging with God and His Word. Rather than fill-in-the-blank questions, SIMPLY BIBLE offers space to be curious and ask your own questions. You will learn to observe, understand, and apply. Don't get me wrong, just like coloring books, traditional Bible studies have their place. Without them, I wouldn't be the Bible student that I am today. And yet, I am rather fond of this SIMPLY BIBLE series. With gentle direction, these books allow quiet spaces for listening to and knowing God, relating with Him by sharing in His story. It is *simply* the Bible.

Since its inception, I've known the joy and privilege of watching others seek God through SIMPLY BIBLE. I've watched these Bible studies become windows into hearts, souls, and minds growing with God. These workbooks tell personal stories. And although the stories are often much too private for me to observe closely, I treasure each one in my heart. If I could, I'd pile them up in my basement. Perhaps it's cheesy, but in some tender way they all pile up in the "basement in my heart."

SO, WELCOME TO **SIMPLY BIBLE!** The rest of the introduction provides step-by-step guidance on getting started with the inductive Bible study method. You'll find everything you need to know to engage directly with God and His Word. Please read these sections *before* beginning the study.

"WHERE IS HE WHO HAS BEEN
BORN KING OF THE JEWS?
FOR WE SAW HIS STAR WHEN
IT ROSE AND HAVE COME TO
WORSHIP HIM."

MATTHEW 2:2

simply bible

AN INDUCTIVE BIBLE STUDY

After her first study, a friend described SIMPLY BIBLE as "leaving behind her paint by numbers set for a blank canvas." Whether painting, drawing, or digging into God's Word, using a blank canvas can be a little intimidating. It takes practice! Just as artists learn particular methods and handle special tools to create a masterpiece, so do Bible study students.

The methodology utilized within SIMPLY BIBLE is known as *inductive study*. This method is used by Bible scholars, pastors, teachers, and students of all levels, and can easily be completed using a Bible and plain notebook. Frankly, the SIMPLY BIBLE workbooks are not necessary for inductive study. However, most readers agree that these user-friendly guides simplify and ease the study process by providing everything needed in one place via an attractive, logical format.

The inductive method involves three basic steps that often overlap with one another:

(1) Observe
(2) Interpret
(3) Apply

This three-step format helps to paint a more thorough understanding of God's Word.

On the following pages, you will find A QUICK START GUIDE TO **SIMPLY BIBLE.** Bookmark and use this as needed. The quick-start guide is followed by a more thorough explanation of the format and basic study tools. Take time to get a feel for each step. Read the examples. And then, dig in!

AND SHE EXCLAIMED WITH A
LOUD CRY, "BLESSED ARE YOU
AMONG WOMEN, AND BLESSED IS
THE FRUIT OF YOUR WOMB!"

LUKE 1:42

getting *started*

A QUICK-START GUIDE

getting *started*

A QUICK-START GUIDE

READ	OBSERVE	INTERPRET
Read the passage. Try some or all of these ideas to help you read carefully. (Highlighters and colored pencils are fun here!)	As you read, write down your observations in this column. Simply notice what the Scripture *says*. This is your place for notes. Ideas include:	In this column, record what the passage *means*.
• Read the passage in a different version.	• Ask questions of the text, like "who, what, when, where, or how."	One way to interpret is to answer any questions asked during observation. Try to first answer these *without* the aid of other helps. Allow Scripture to explain Scripture. It often does.
• Read it out loud.	• Jot down key items: people, places, things. Mark places on a map.	If the answers are not intuitive or easily found near the passage, other tools are available. Use boxes A, B, and C to identify a key word, define it, and look up a cross reference. This extra research will shed light on the meaning.
• Underline, circle, box, or highlight repeated words, unfamiliar words, or anything that pricks your heart or catches your attention.	• Ask, "What does this passage say about God? Jesus? Holy Spirit?"	
• Listen to the passage while running errands.	• Note what took place before and after this passage.	IMPORTANT: *Seek to understand what Scripture meant to the original readers (or hearers). Try to see and look at the world through the eyes of the ancient Israelites, the early church, or the Greco-Roman culture of the day.*
• Doodle or write out a verse in your workbook or a journaling Bible.	• Ponder.	
	• Ask God if there is anything else He'd like you to notice.	

PLEASE NOTE: The following sections (labeled A, B, and C) are interpretation tools. These are meant to be used in unison with the INTERPRET column on the previous page to aid in interpreting Scripture. Most students find it helpful to complete these *before* interpreting. Consider this your toolbox. Find what's most helpful for you.

A KEY WORDS	**B** DEFINITIONS	**C** CROSS REFERENCES
When you notice a word that is repeated multiple times, unfamiliar, or interesting to you in any other way, record it here.	Record definitions of your key words. You can find the appropriate definitions by using: • a Bible concordance (defines words according to the original language) • a Bible dictionary • another translation	Note cross references. This is a solid way to allow Scripture to interpret Scripture. If your Bible does not include cross references, no worries! These tools are easily accessible at Bible websites such as: • blueletterbible.org • biblegateway.com • biblehub.com

MAIN POINT(S)	APPLY
Summarize the main point(s) or note any themes you encountered in the passage.	Apply God's Word to your life. Reflect on how you will think or live differently as a result of studying this passage.

PRAY

Write a short prayer here. When we take time to write something down, that message becomes more etched on our heart. Take a moment to simply be with God. He is why we study. Savor. Know. Praise. Confess. Thank. Ask. Love. Adore. Then carry a nugget of His Word in your heart to ponder and proclaim throughout your day.

"FOR NOTHING WILL BE
IMPOSSIBLE WITH GOD."

LUKE 1:37

step by step

UNPACKING THE INDUCTIVE METHOD

step by *step*

UNPACKING THE INDUCTIVE METHOD

STEP 1: OBSERVE | *See what the Bible **says***.

The first step of Bible study is to observe God's Word.

In our hurried, scurried pace of life, we read too fast, often plowing through the words without taking time to ponder and think about what we're reading. *Observation* helps us to slow down and take notice in order to see. In this first step, we answer, "What does the Bible *say*?"

Have you ever stopped to truly examine and enjoy a piece of art? Artists develop an amazing knack or ability to capture a particular scene, whether real or imagined, onto a blank canvas. How? Artists specialize in *observing* details: setting, color, texture, time, characters, lighting, movement…the list of details is nearly limitless.

We can too.

When my children were younger, blank sketch books and new drawing pencils equaled a special treat. With fresh, new artist tools in hand and a sunny day, my little ones and I would traipse excitedly through a park. Before pulling out a pencil to begin creating, we needed to find the right spot for observing. (I highly recommend that for Bible study, too!)

To observe means "to see, watch, notice, or regard with attention, especially so as to see or learn something."[1] *Especially so as to see or learn something.*

---

[1] **observe**. Dictionary.com. *Dictionary.com Unabridged.* Random House, Inc. http://www.dictionary.com/browse/observe (accessed: March 16, 2018).

And so, my children and I would notice things. Lots of things…the different types of leaves, flowers, plants, grass, insects, animals, and more. Once engaged in observing, details would begin to arise! How fun to zero in and observe the ladybug crawling along the blade of grass or the spots that adorn a toad sunning on the sidewalk or the veins that run throughout a maple leaf. There's so much to see!

Observation implies being curious. Noticing details. Asking questions.

Kids do this naturally. We can too. Be curious with God's Word. Scripture is full of details to notice and numerous questions to ask. When we slow down and take time to "smell the roses" within Scripture, we see and learn.

If you don't relate to art or being a kid again, then consider detective work.

Inductive study is much like detective work. Detectives are trained to observe and notice details. They exude curiosity and examine cases by asking questions: who, what, when, where, how, and why.

Like detectives, we use observation skills too. Intuitively, without even thinking about it, we observe and interpret life around us.

Using simple observation, we discern whether a loved one comes home happy, sad, or mad. After all, there's a huge difference between walking through the door with a smile or a frown. Singing a tune versus grumbling. Dancing versus slamming doors. We notice the "signs." And because we care, we ask questions. Inquisitive minds want to know, "What's up?" This leads to more questions: "Really? How? Why? Where? When? Who? Are you okay?"

You get the picture.

Detective work transfers to reading and understanding God's Word. Observation means we read, study, and ask questions of the text. We look to see, "What does the Scripture say?" If short on time, we simply ask, "What does the Scripture say about who God is?"

As you read, pray and talk with God about His Word. Ask Him to help you see. Ask Him questions about the text. Highlight verses that touch your heart. If anything is especially noteworthy to you, jot it down in the space labeled OBSERVE in your workbook. (Keep in mind: the SIMPLY BIBLE framework is just a guide. You choose to fill in as little or as much as you desire.)

Observation ideas include:

1. Highlight or journal a verse that pops out to you.
2. Write down your observations.
3. Go back and read it again while asking questions of the text. Write out your questions.
4. Play detective and ask, "Who, what, when, where, how, or why?"
5. Note what took place before and after this passage.
6. Notice repeated or unfamiliar words. In your workbook, underline, circle, box, or highlight these words. (This is *your* place for notes.)
7. Look for people and places.
8. Mark places on a map.
9. Ponder.
10. Ask God if there is anything else He'd like for you to notice.

The bottom line? Read. Read carefully. Observe at least one thing, particularly something about God Himself. This allows us to see Scripture more clearly.

STEP 2: INTERPRET | *Understand what the Scripture **means**.*

After careful observation of a landscape, an artist sketches an interpretation of what he sees onto the canvas. Observation and interpretation go hand in hand. A circle is a circle. A square is a square. As closely as possible, the artist defines and places an image of what he observes onto the canvas. Careful observation leads to a life-like rendering such that the viewer will understand what the artist himself observed.

The same is true of the Bible. Observation and interpretation go hand in hand. Scripture will often interpret Scripture. As we carefully read and observe what the Scripture says, we frequently understand and simultaneously interpret its *meaning*. So within our daily study format, observation and interpretation are located side-by-side.

One simple way to understand the meaning of Scripture is to answer the questions we asked in the observation process: who, what, where, when, how, and why. Try to answer these questions without the aid of study notes or other helps. Utilize Scripture to interpret Scripture. Often, the answer is readily available.

Other times, interpretation is not so easy. After all, the Bible was written in ancient times, spanning the course of over two thousand years, *by* a people and *to* a people of a culture that is utterly foreign to us.

Therefore, certain resources are handy. These tools can help us to place and understand Scripture in its original context in order to properly interpret. (Think of an artist using a ruler—a simple tool that helps to more accurately reproduce a scene. A ruler is not necessary, but is useful.)

Bible study tools can include:
- *Cross references:* Cross references allow us to use nearby or related passages to more accurately interpret Scripture.
- *Bible dictionaries or concordances:* These tools allow us to understand the meaning of a word in its original language.
- *Bible handbooks and commentaries:* Resources like these help us to verify our conclusions as well as provide historical or cultural context.

It's important to remember that Scripture, in its original context, had only one meaning, not multiple meanings. And although our God can be mysterious in His ways, there are no mystical or hidden meanings within either Genesis or Luke. Both Moses and Luke wrote a specific message, at a specific time, and in a specific place, for a specific group of people. Each author meant what he said. For this study, we want to know what Moses and Luke meant and how the original hearers understood their words. Although we may not always be able to determine an author's specific intent, that is our goal.

Interpretation implies understanding. The originally intended meaning and its context are important. Be reasonable. Compare.

Seek correct answers, but give yourself grace. A child's rendering of a ladybug on a blade of grass will not equate to Van Gogh's renderings, and yet, there is something wholly precious about the works of a child. Our renderings of Scripture won't ever equate to a Bible scholar's commentary. That is not our goal. Our goal is knowing and enjoying God. Sometimes this involves taking tiny baby steps in His direction.

A, B, & C: TOOLS FOR INTERPRETATION

If the answers are not intuitive or easily found within the passage, tools are available to help us better understand. Our daily lesson format provides three boxes intended to support interpretation. Here, you'll find space to identify key words, define those key words, and record supporting verses (cross references). These are intended to help and guide you as you interpret Scripture. Consider this to be your interpretation toolbox. Use the tools however you find them to be helpful.

> **A.** KEY WORDS | Did you notice that a word was repeated, seems important, is unfamiliar, or interests you in any way? Record it here.
>
> **B.** DEFINITIONS | Use this box to record definitions of the words you listed. To find definitions:
>
> • *Read the verse using a different Bible translation.* This can be a simple way to define a word. For example, our practice lesson (on page 32) notes the word *apostle* from I Timothy 1:1. The ESV says "apostle," while the Amplified Bible expounds: "apostle (special messenger, personally chosen representative)." [1]
>
> • *Use a Bible concordance.* This book looks at words in their original language. I like the **Strong's Concordance**, which can also be found online.

---

[1] The Holy Bible: The Amplified Bible. 1987. La Habra, CA: The Lockman Foundation.

i. Going online? Try **Blue Letter Bible**, a free web-based concordance.

ii. Once there, (referring to our practice lesson on page 30) simply type "I Timothy 1" into the *Search the Bible* box. Select the box called *Tools* next to I Timothy 1 and a menu appears. Find and select the corresponding Strong's Concordance number for "apostle" (in this case: G652). Click on it. You'll retrieve the Greek word, original definitions, and how it is used in other places of the Bible. It's fascinating! Make note of the definitions you find.

• *Try a Bible dictionary.* In order to define people or locate places, Bible dictionaries are handy.

i. Online, try **Bible Gateway, Blue Letter Bible,** or **Bible Hub.**

ii. Wonderful Bible study apps exist, too. For example, the **Bible Map** app is simple-to-use and automatically syncs Scripture with maps.

C. CROSS REFERENCES | Many Bibles offer cross references. This is a rock-solid way to allow Scripture to interpret Scripture. If your Bible does not include cross references (most journaling Bibles do not), no worries! Accessing cross references online is easy. **Blue Letter Bible** or **Bible Hub** are great places to start.

Still not sure?

Note your question and talk to God about it. Ponder. As we ponder Scripture, God often illuminates our understanding. Other times, He allows certain things to remain unanswered. His ways are sometimes beyond our ways and our understanding. Ultimately, we walk by faith.

Remember to share and discuss your questions with others at Bible study. Studying God's Word is meant to be done in a community where we learn and grow together in knowing, understanding, and loving God.

WANT MORE? Our daily study format includes space for definitions and cross references. However, there are other Bible study resources available if you'd like to dig even deeper.

Bible commentaries are written by biblical scholars. These books provide cultural and historical context while commenting on Scripture verse-by-verse.

Personally, I admire the dedication and genius of scholars who write commentaries. These dedicated people study for the glory of God. And yet, I recommend saving their wonderful resources as a last step. Why? Because commentaries are not a substitute for reading, understanding, and engaging God's Word on your own. First seek to understand God's Word without a commentary. Then, if desired, utilize a commentary for double checking your work.

Also, please note that commentaries are written according to various theological perspectives. It is helpful to compare them and to know your sources. This is especially crucial if roaming the Internet. Please surf with discernment and great care. I can't emphasize this enough. Unfortunately, even commentaries found on popular Bible study sites are not always researched and written by trained biblical scholars. If unsure, background check the author's credentials. Bible degrees and scholastic training from accredited universities and institutions are important.

To find reliable Biblical commentaries, I recommend:

www.bestcommentaries.com   **www.challies.com**

SUMMARIZE: Your daily lesson framework offers space for you to summarize and identify the main point(s) of the Bible passage that you've read. Understanding the main idea of a passage helps to ensure correct interpretation before moving into application.

STEP 3: APPLY | *Put it all **together.***

Here's the "so what?" How will I think or act differently because of God's Word? With the Holy Spirit's help, observation and interpretation lead us to better understand the meaning of a Bible passage. That's thrilling! Discovering a nugget of truth, a promise, or a revelation about God Himself takes my breath away and inevitably leads me to praise and worship Him. There is no other book like the Bible:

> For the word of God is living and active,
> sharper than any two-edged sword,
> piercing to the division of soul and of spirit,
> of joints and of marrow, and discerning the
> thoughts and intentions of the heart.
>
> HEBREWS 4:12

The God of the Universe loves us and personally reveals Himself through His living Word. When He does, it cuts in a good way. Then we're ready to *apply* His Word to our everyday lives…to think and act differently.

APPLICATION IS THE CREATIVE PART. Yes, the original authors of Scripture had a particular meaning in mind, but the personal applications of Scripture are many. This step is between you and God. If a specific verse, word, or idea strikes a chord in your heart, *slow down.* Take note. Ponder. Show God the discovery. This is the amazing process of God revealing Himself and His truths to you through His Word and the power of His Holy Spirit.

God looks at our hearts. He sees, knows, and loves His sheep, and so He may use His Word to teach, correct, rebuke, or train. He is always equipping.(II Timothy 3:16-17) If you're willing, God will lead you to apply His Word specifically and personally to your own everyday life.

Application ideas include:

1. Worship God for who He is according to a truth or promise discovered.
2. Thank Him for a lesson learned.
3. Note an example to follow.
4. Confess a sin revealed.
5. Pray a prayer.
6. Obey, trust, and follow God's way, His command, His plan.
7. Memorize a verse.

Bottom line? Ask, "How will I think or act differently because of what I've learned in God's Word?"

WRAPPING UP: PRAY | *Respond to a **Holy God**.*

Application implies a recognition of who God is. And so when wrapping up Bible study, the application step nearly always leads me to bow my heart in worship, confession, thanksgiving, or petition. Accordingly, the SIMPLY BIBLE daily format includes a place for *prayer*. Please use this! It may be the most important step of all.

Enjoy a lingering moment of being with God in His Word. Savor. Learn. Grow. Know. Thank. Praise. Confess. Yield. Love. Then carry a nugget of truth in your heart to ponder as you go about your day.

lesson *samples*

PRACTICE LESSONS & EXAMPLES

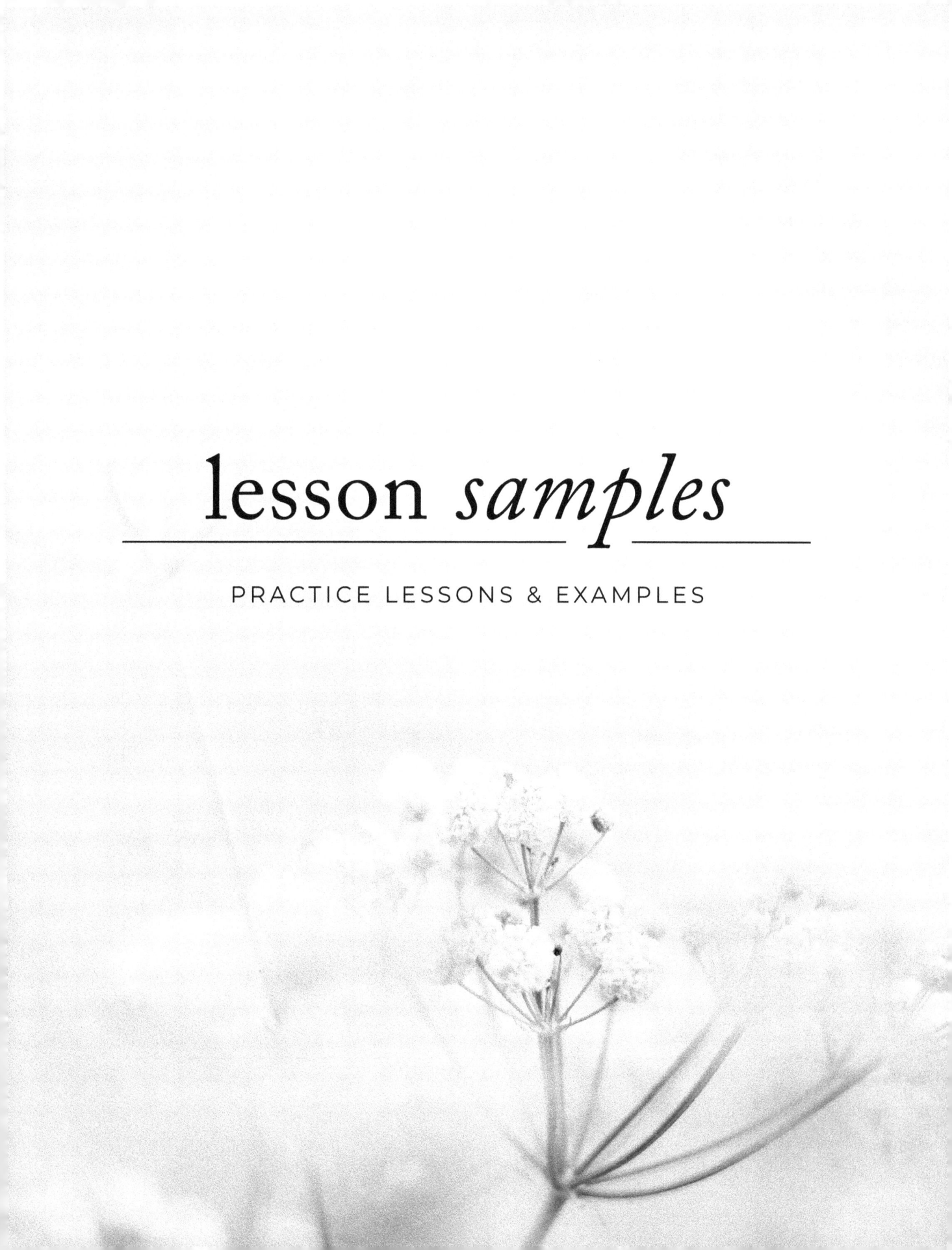

practice *lesson*

I TIMOTHY 1:1-2

NOW IT'S YOUR TURN! Give it try. Below are two verses, I Timothy 1:1-2. As you read, feel free to highlight, circle, underline and mark up the text in whatever way you like. In the *Observe* column, jot down details that pop out to you and write down questions that come to mind. Then *Interpret*. Simply use the Scripture passage itself or hop over to the tool kit: *Key Words, Definitions,* and *Cross References.* Use these as previously discussed to help you better understand the meaning of the passage. Finish by summarizing, applying, and praying.

This is your workbook. The intent is for you to journal your thoughts as you engage with God and His Word. Don't be shy. Be you, be with God, and enjoy!

READ	OBSERVE	INTERPRET
Paul, an apostle of Christ Jesus by command of God our Savior and of Christ Jesus our hope, ² To Timothy, my true child in the faith: Grace, mercy, and peace from God the Father and Christ Jesus our Lord.		

KEY WORDS	DEFINITIONS	CROSS REFERENCES

MAIN POINT(S)	APPLY

PRAY

sample *lesson*

I TIMOTHY 1:1-2 | FOR THOSE CRAZY, BUSY DAYS

We're busy. Life can be hectic. Some days you just don't have time to go deep in your study. That's okay. One truth from God's Word transforms hearts, which often transforms the day. Using I Timothy 1:1-2, here's what a study might look like with very little time. The goal is to observe, interpret, and apply just **one thing** (particularly about who God is):

READ	OBSERVE	INTERPRET
Paul, an apostle of Christ Jesus by command of God our Savior and of Christ Jesus our hope, ² To Timothy, my true child in the faith: Grace, mercy, and peace from God the Father and Christ Jesus our Lord.	Christ Jesus is mentioned 3 times. According to Paul, who is he?	Jesus is "our hope." He is "our Lord." He commanded Paul to be his apostle. He gives grace, mercy, and peace.

KEY WORDS	DEFINITIONS	CROSS REFERENCES
apostle	a special messenger, a personally chosen representative (Amplified Bible)	I Timothy 1:12 I thank him who has given me strength, Christ Jesus our Lord because he judged me faithful, appointing me to his service…

MAIN POINT(S)

The apostle Paul greets Timothy in a letter.

APPLY

Even in his greeting of a letter, Paul brings glory to Jesus and reminds Timothy of the hope we have in Him. How can I greet others with this same exuberance for Christ throughout my day today? This glorifies Jesus and is good for me and others.

PRAY

Lord God, thank You for today's reminder of hope. I praise You, Jesus, for You are Lord. Thank You for Your gifts of grace, mercy, and peace. Like Paul, please help me and my loved ones to be vessels of Your hope, grace, mercy, and peace today.

sample *lesson*

I TIMOTHY 1:1-2 | GOING DEEPER

Do you have time to linger in God's Word? Using I Timothy 1:1-2, here's an example of what a more extensive study could look like. Observe as much or as little as you like. Remember: no two journals will look the same.

READ	OBSERVE	INTERPRET
Paul, an apostle of Christ Jesus by command of God our Savior and of Christ Jesus our hope, ²To Timothy, my true child in the faith: Grace, mercy, and peace from God the Father and Christ Jesus our Lord.	Who is Paul? What is an apostle? Christ Jesus is mentioned 3 times in two verses! Who is He? Why is He our hope? Who is Timothy? Paul refers to Timothy as "my" true child. Why? Faith in what? Is it common to offer grace, mercy, and peace in a greeting? Notice Paul distinguishes between God the Father and Jesus Christ.	Paul: an apostle of Jesus. Apostle: chosen by God. Jesus is our hope and our Lord. He commanded Paul to be His apostle. He gives grace, mercy, and peace. Christ is our Savior. He is also in us." (Col. 1:27) Timothy: Paul's true child in the faith. Not sure why Paul uses this phrase. Perhaps Paul witnessed and was part of Timothy's spiritual birth. According to Philippians 2:2, they labored together as "father and son." Faith: belief in Christ Mercy is found in other greetings, but the combination is unique for Paul to include in his letters.

KEY WORDS	DEFINITIONS	CROSS REFERENCES
apostle	a special messenger, a personally chosen representative (Amplified Bible)	I Timothy 1:12 I thank him who has given me strength, Christ Jesus our Lord because he judged me faithful, appointing me to his service…
hope	an expectation	Colossians 1:27 To them God chose to make known how great among the Gentiles are the riches of the glory of this mystery, which is Christ in you, the hope of glory.
true child of the faith		Titus 1:4 To Titus, my true child in a common faith

MAIN POINT(S)

The apostle Paul greets Timothy in a letter.

APPLY

Even in a greeting, Paul brings glory to Jesus and reminds Timothy of the hope we have in Him. How can I greet others with this same exuberance for Christ? What am I doing to "give birth" to children of the faith? Praise God for His grace, peace, and mercy! Am I extending this to others?

PRAY

Lord God, thank You for today's reminder of hope. I praise You, Jesus, for You are Lord. Thank You for Your gifts of grace, mercy, and peace. Like Paul, please help me and my loved ones to be vessels of Your hope, grace, mercy, and peace today. Lord, I pray for _____ to become a true child of yours. Please open her heart to receive your grace and peace. Please open doors for me to share with her in words and actions.

AND MARY SAID,
"BEHOLD, I AM THE SERVANT
OF THE LORD; LET IT BE TO ME
ACCORDING TO YOUR WORD."

LUKE 1:38

YOU DID IT! That's it. That's all there is to the **SIMPLY BIBLE** inductive process. If this is your first time, the process may feel a little awkward at first. Don't worry. You probably don't remember how clumsy and time consuming it was the very first time you tried tying your shoe, riding a bike, or driving a car. Practice helps. The same will be true for Bible study. Like riding a bicycle, it gets easier.

Likewise, please know that your study guide will look different from most others. You are unique and special, and so your observations and application will be unique. Every artist creates something different with a "blank page."

Indeed, you've probably gathered by now that this study is different, and different often falls outside of our comfort zones. The purpose of this Bible study is that you may confidently read, understand, and apply God's Word like you've never before experienced using *simply* the Bible.

IT WILL REQUIRE A COMMITMENT. Would you please commit to finishing this study book? By the end, with consistency, perseverance, and time spent with Him, you will better know God, His Word, and your identity in Him.

You're more observant, smarter, and stronger than you think you are. God created you that way. He desires to be known. He wants to show you that you are loved, valued, and never alone. Lean into Him. Ask, seek, and you will find. His grace is sufficient. His power is made perfect in our weakness.

> As the rain and the snow come down from
> heaven, and do not return to it without
> watering the earth and making it bud and
> flourish, so that it yields seed for the sower
> and bread for the eater,

so is my word that goes out from my
mouth: It will not return to me empty, but
will accomplish what I desire and achieve
the purpose for which I sent it.

You will go out in joy and be led forth in
peace; the mountains and hills will burst
into song before you, and all the trees of
the field will clap their hands.

ISAIAH 55:10-12

Lord, thank You for Your Word! Like rain and snow watering the earth so that it might bud and flourish, may Your Word now water our hearts, minds, and souls, that our love for You and for one another would bud and flourish. May Your purposes and desires be accomplished. As we study with You, may we go out in joy and be led forth in Your peace. With all creation may we sing and clap for joy and bring glory to Your Name...

in *context*

EXAMINING THE CONTEXT OF **EVE & MARY**

in *context*

EXAMINING THE CONTEXT OF **EVE & MARY**

The SIMPLY BIBLE Study of Eve and Mary will delve into both the Old and New Testaments. To look at Eve, we will peer into the first book of the Old Testament, Genesis. Eve's story is found in the first four chapters. For Mary, we will jump over to the New Testament. Although each gospel writer mentions Mary, Luke has the most to say about her, so we will primarily focus on his account of the good news of Jesus. However, we will also examine Matthew's writing on Mary and a unique story about her that only John shares in his gospel account.

All portions of Scripture within this study fall into the category of biblical narrative, meaning these stories are about real places, people, and events. Most importantly, these stories tell us something about who God is. His story begins in Genesis. The creation account recorded in Genesis provides a theological understanding of God and, subsequently, the first people to inhabit the earth. Genesis is not a science book. We will not learn how to make a universe and all its living creatures. Instead, we seek to know God and the first humans He created, Adam and Eve. To do so, we need to "put on our ancient Near East (ANE) glasses" and seek to understand how the Israelites understood the creation account. Many scholars believe that the first five books of the Bible were originally written by Moses. So how did Moses and God's people of that day, the Israelites, understand and interpret God's words?

Similarly, for the New Testament gospel accounts, we want to put ourselves in the shoes of those who walked the Roman roads of the day. The world at that time differs greatly from the world of Genesis 1-4 or the world we live in today. Let's slip on our sandals, and get our feet a little dusty as we journey with Mary. Let's put on our first-century glasses to see the world through her eyes. What was life like in Judea at this time? How is life different from the 21st-century culture in which we find ourselves? How is it the same? We want to understand the first-century Greco-Roman context as much as we can.

To further understand how the historical contexts of the Old and New Testaments enable us to accurately observe and interpret the Bible, I recommend *How to Study the Bible for All It's Worth* by Gordon D. Fee and Douglas Stuart.

Though their historical contexts differ, we can approach Old and New Testament narratives similarly. For our purposes, I will offer three simple rules to keep in mind when studying narrative passages in Scripture:

1. GOD IS THE HERO OF THE STORY.

The Hero of the biblical narrative is God Himself. As we approach Scripture to understand these women better, let us remember the real purpose of the stories: to know God Himself. I encourage you to always ask, "What do I learn abou God from this passage?"

2. READ LITERALLY.

As mentioned before, these are real places, people, and events that occurred at a specific time and place. So read not symbolically or metaphorically, but literally.

3. LOOK FOR THE SPIRITUAL LESSON.

- Look for the lessons in this book that surpass culture and are for all time. The Bible holds lessons that remain just as important and applicable for us living in the 21st century as for those in the 1st century. These are the lessons to carry with us in our hearts and minds. God transforms us through them.

One important caveat affects how we read Genesis 1—it is written poetically. Hebrew poetry was not intended to be read literally. Yet, Genesis 1 uniquely describes God's creation of the world through the literary genre of ancient cosmology. This chapter provides Moses's historical perspective through the means of ancient Near Eastern literary techniques/methods. It is as if he put history into music lyrics or a poem. For our study on Eve and Mary, focus on reading Genesis 1 to learn more about God and why He created the world.

REMEMBER THAT BIBLE STUDY IS NOT ROCKET SCIENCE.
God would not ask us to know Him through the Bible and then make studying the Bible impossible. As you study, use common sense. A text could never mean what it never meant to its author or the original hearers.

Finally, let go of assumptions, presuppositions, and church traditions. This is a fancy way to say let go of what you think you know. This is difficult, especially if you grew up in the church or have done numerous Bible studies. The challenge, therefore, is to read God's Word with fresh eyes as if reading for the first time, putting on our first-century glasses only after removing our 21st-century glasses. Again, put yourself in the shoes of the author and his readers.

Following these simple rules will help us better observe, interpret, and apply the Bible to our everyday lives. More importantly, using this approach allows us to know the God of the Bible better.

a *challenge*

PONDER

a *challenge*

One of my favorite verses about Mary is found in Luke chapter two:

> But Mary treasured up all these things,
> pondering them in her heart.
>
> LUKE 2:19

We will dig into this verse more within our study, but let's unpack it a bit here. My Bible dictionary tells me that to treasure means to store up mentally and preserve knowledge and memories for later use. Mary treasured up all these things not only in her mind, but Luke tells us she pondered them in her heart. To ponder is to meditate, to reflect deeply on a subject. What did Mary ponder? All these things, meaning all the things she was witnessing, learning, and experiencing about Jesus from the unique perspective of being his mom and then follower.

What a beautiful example Mary provides! In our busy lives and self-absorbed worlds, we often neglect deep thinking and meditating on Jesus and His Word. So, pondering will be the ultimate challenge for us in this study.

I challenge you to take two minutes before and after each day's study to ponder Jesus. Two minutes to ponder before. Two minutes to ponder after. Be quiet and be with Him. His Spirit is near. There is no need to write or do anything for this challenge unless you want to. Our workbooks provide plenty of space for more notes or prayer. Whatever your approach, practice God's presence. Practice being with Him and listening to Him. Little by little, we, too, will treasure what we learn about Jesus as we study. These treasures are worth stockpiling.

AND BLESSED IS SHE WHO
BELIEVED THAT THERE
WOULD BE A FULFILLMENT
OF WHAT WAS SPOKEN TO
HER FROM THE LORD.

LUKE 1:45

AND GOD SAW EVERYTHING
THAT HE HAD MADE, AND
BEHOLD, IT WAS VERY GOOD.

GENESIS 1:31

chapter *one*

GENESIS 1

take *note*

NOTES ON GENESIS 1

take *note*

NOTES ON GENESIS 1

day *one*

GENESIS 1:1-5

READ	OBSERVE	INTERPRET
[1] In the beginning, God created the heavens and the earth. [2] The earth was without form and void, and darkness was over the face of the deep. And the Spirit of God was hovering over the face of the waters. [3] And God said, "Let there be light," and there was light. [4] And God saw that the light was good. And God separated the light from the darkness. [5] God called the light Day, and the darkness he called Night. And there was evening and there was morning, the first day.		

KEY WORDS	DEFINITIONS	CROSS REFERENCES

MAIN POINT(S)	APPLY

PRAY

day *two*

READ

⁶ And God said, "Let there be an expanse in the midst of the waters, and let it separate the waters from the waters." ⁷ And God made the expanse and separated the waters that were under the expanse from the waters that were above the expanse. And it was so. ⁸ And God called the expanse Heaven. And there was evening and there was morning, the second day.

⁹ And God said, "Let the waters under the heavens be gathered together into one place, and let the dry land appear." And it was so. ¹⁰ God called the dry land Earth, and the waters that were gathered together he called Seas. And God saw that it was good.

¹¹ And God said, "Let the earth sprout vegetation, plants yielding seed, and fruit trees bearing fruit in which is their seed, each according to its kind, on the earth." And it was so. ¹² The earth brought forth vegetation, plants yielding seed according to their own kinds, and trees bearing fruit in which is their seed, each according to its kind. And God saw that it was good. ¹³ And there was evening and there was morning, the third day.

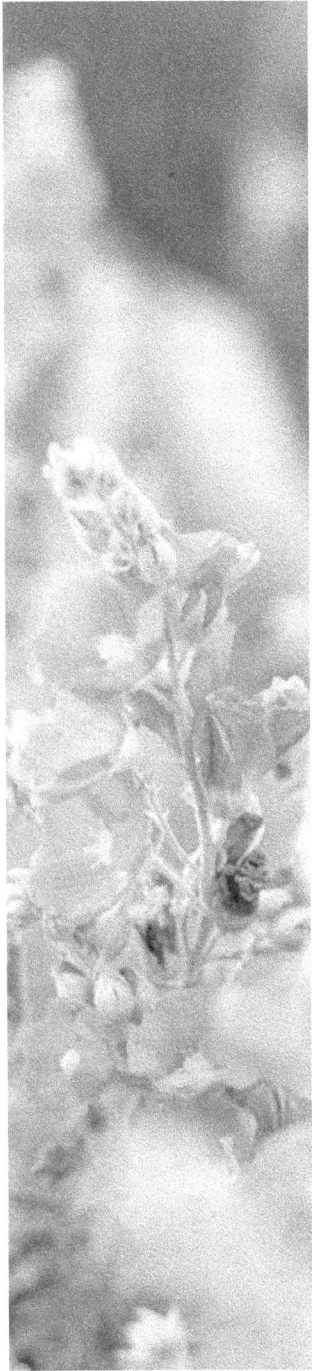

OBSERVE	INTERPRET

KEY WORDS	DEFINITIONS	CROSS REFERENCES

MAIN POINT(S)	APPLY

PRAY

IN THE BEGINNING, GOD
CREATED THE HEAVENS
AND THE EARTH.

GENESIS 1:1

day *three*

GENESIS 1:14-25

READ

[14] And God said, "Let there be lights in the expanse of the heavens to separate the day from the night. And let them be for signs and for seasons, and for days and years, [15] and let them be lights in the expanse of the heavens to give light upon the earth." And it was so. [16] And God made the two great lights—the greater light to rule the day and the lesser light to rule the night—and the stars. [17] And God set them in the expanse of the heavens to give light on the earth, [18] to rule over the day and over the night, and to separate the light from the darkness. And God saw that it was good. [19] And there was evening and there was morning, the fourth day.

[20] And God said, "Let the waters swarm with swarms of living creatures, and let birds fly above the earth across the expanse of the heavens." [21] So God created the great sea creatures and every living creature that moves, with which the waters swarm, according to their kinds, and every winged bird according to its kind. And God saw that it was good. [22] And God blessed them, saying, "Be fruitful and multiply and fill the waters in the seas, and let birds multiply on the earth." [23] And there was evening and there was morning, the fifth day.

[24] And God said, "Let the earth bring forth living creatures according to their kinds—livestock and creeping things and beasts of the earth according to their kinds." And it was so. [25] And God made the beasts of the earth according to their kinds and the livestock according to their kinds, and everything that creeps on the ground according to its kind. And God saw that it was good.

OBSERVE	INTERPRET

KEY WORDS	DEFINITIONS	CROSS REFERENCES

MAIN POINT(S)	APPLY

PRAY

AND GOD SAID,
"LET THERE BE LIGHT," AND
THERE WAS LIGHT.

GENESIS 1:3

day *four*

READ

²⁶ Then God said, "Let us make man in our image, after our likeness. And let them have dominion over the fish of the sea and over the birds of the heavens and over the livestock and over all the earth and over every creeping thing that creeps on the earth."

²⁷ So God created man in his own image, in the image of God he created him; male and female he created them.

²⁸ And God blessed them. And God said to them, "Be fruitful and multiply and fill the earth and subdue it, and have dominion over the fish of the sea and over the birds of the heavens and over every living thing that moves on the earth." ²⁹ And God said, "Behold, I have given you every plant yielding seed that is on the face of all the earth, and every tree with seed in its fruit. You shall have them for food. ³⁰ And to every beast of the earth and to every bird of the heavens and to everything that creeps on the earth, everything that has the breath of life, I have given every green plant for food." And it was so. ³¹ And God saw everything that he had made, and behold, it was very good. And there was evening and there was morning, the sixth day.

OBSERVE	INTERPRET

KEY WORDS	DEFINITIONS	CROSS REFERENCES

MAIN POINT(S)	APPLY

PRAY

AND THE RIB THAT THE LORD
GOD HAD TAKEN FROM THE MAN
HE MADE INTO A WOMAN AND
BROUGHT HER TO THE MAN.

GENESIS 2:22

day *five*

GENESIS 1 | REVIEW AND DISCUSSION QUESTIONS

1 Summarize this week's passage.	2 Write out your favorite verse, perhaps in your own words.
3 Share significant observations concerning creation.	4 How does God create light? What do you learn about God's Word?
5 If God can speak light into darkness, how might this encourage you today?	6 What did you learn about Eve this week?

7 According to Genesis 1, why was Eve created? Does her purpose differ from Adam's? Explain.

8 How does Adam and Eve's purpose relate to you? Apply.

9 How does God summarize His creation after creating man and woman?

10 Explain God's view of humans. Explain how this applies to you.

11 What did you learn about God this week?

12 Ponder and praise God. Thank Him for the lessons you have learned.

take it to *heart*

USE THIS SPACE TO WRITE OUT OR JOURNAL A FAVORITE
VERSE OR PASSAGE FROM THIS WEEK'S STUDY

"IT IS NOT GOOD THAT THE MAN SHOULD BE ALONE; I WILL MAKE HIM A HELPER FIT FOR HIM."

GENESIS 2:18

chapter *two*

GENESIS 2

take *note*

NOTES ON GENESIS 2

take *note*

day *one*

READ	OBSERVE	INTERPRET
[1] Thus the heavens and the earth were finished, and all the host of them. [2] And on the seventh day God finished his work that he had done, and he rested on the seventh day from all his work that he had done. [3] So God blessed the seventh day and made it holy, because on it God rested from all his work that he had done in creation.		

KEY WORDS	DEFINITIONS	CROSS REFERENCES

MAIN POINT(S)	APPLY

PRAY

day *two*

READ

⁴ These are the generations of the heavens and the earth when they were created, in the day that the Lord God made the earth and the heavens.

⁵ When no bush of the field was yet in the land and no small plant of the field had yet sprung up—for the Lord God had not caused it to rain on the land, and there was no man to work the ground, ⁶ and a mist was going up from the land and was watering the whole face of the ground— ⁷ then the Lord God formed the man of dust from the ground and breathed into his nostrils the breath of life, and the man became a living creature. ⁸ And the Lord God planted a garden in Eden, in the east, and there he put the man whom he had formed. ⁹ And out of the ground the Lord God made to spring up every tree that is pleasant to the sight and good for food. The tree of life was in the midst of the garden, and the tree of the knowledge of good and evil.

¹⁰ A river flowed out of Eden to water the garden, and there it divided and became four rivers. ¹¹ The name of the first is the Pishon. It is the one that flowed around the whole land of Havilah, where there is gold. ¹² And the gold of that land is good; bdellium and onyx stone are there. ¹³ The name of the second river is the Gihon. It is the one that flowed around the whole land of Cush. ¹⁴ And the name of the third river is the Tigris, which flows east of Assyria. And the fourth river is the Euphrates.

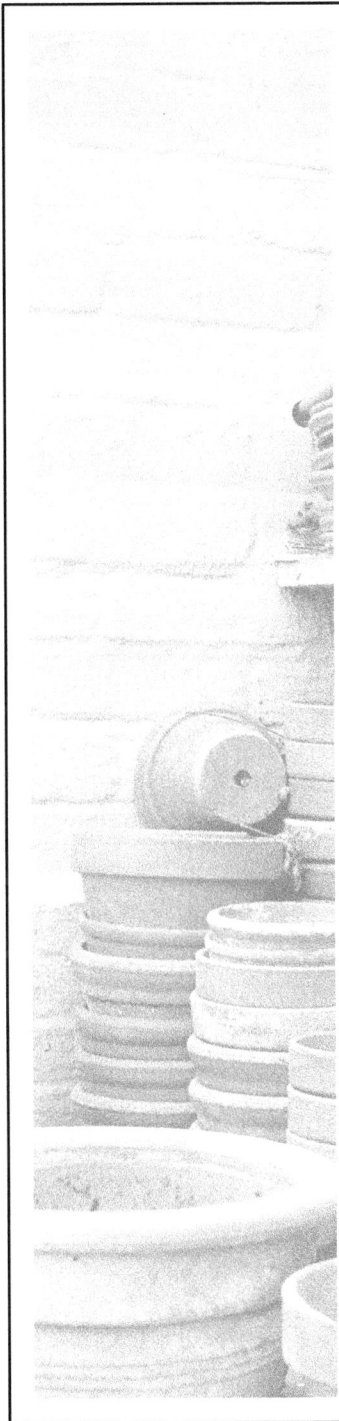

	OBSERVE	INTERPRET

KEY WORDS	DEFINITIONS	CROSS REFERENCES

MAIN POINT(S)	APPLY

PRAY

AND THE RIB THAT THE LORD
GOD HAD TAKEN FROM
THE MAN HE MADE INTO A
WOMAN AND BROUGHT HER
TO THE MAN.

GENESIS 2:22

day *three*

GENESIS 2:15-20

READ

¹⁵ The Lord God took the man and put him in the garden of Eden to work it and keep it. ¹⁶ And the Lord God commanded the man, saying, "You may surely eat of every tree of the garden, ¹⁷ but of the tree of the knowledge of good and evil you shall not eat, for in the day that you eat of it you shall surely die."

¹⁸ Then the Lord God said, "It is not good that the man should be alone; I will make him a helper fit for him." ¹⁹ Now out of the ground the Lord God had formed every beast of the field and every bird of the heavens and brought them to the man to see what he would call them. And whatever the man called every living creature, that was its name. ²⁰ The man gave names to all livestock and to the birds of the heavens and to every beast of the field. But for Adam there was not found a helper fit for him.

OBSERVE

INTERPRET

KEY WORDS	DEFINITIONS	CROSS REFERENCES

MAIN POINT(S)	APPLY

PRAY

day *four*

GENESIS 2:21-25

READ

²¹ So the Lord God caused a deep sleep to fall upon the man, and while he slept took one of his ribs and closed up its place with flesh. ²² And the rib that the Lord God had taken from the man he made into a woman and brought her to the man. ²³ Then the man said,

"This at last is bone of my bones
    and flesh of my flesh;
she shall be called Woman,
    because she was taken out of Man."

²⁴ Therefore a man shall leave his father and his mother and hold fast to his wife, and they shall become one flesh. ²⁵ And the man and his wife were both naked and were not ashamed.

OBSERVE

INTERPRET

KEY WORDS	DEFINITIONS	CROSS REFERENCES

MAIN POINT(S)	APPLY

PRAY

day *five*

GENESIS 2 | REVIEW AND DISCUSSION QUESTIONS

1 Summarize this week's passage.	2 Write out your favorite verse, perhaps in your own words.
3 Share your insights about God from verses 1-3 and their implications for your own life.	4 Share all you learned about Adam. Where did God put him, and why?
5 Describe the garden.	6 What did you learn about Eve this week?

7 Does Genesis 2 change Eve's created purpose from Chapter 1? What additional role does Eve have? Explain.

8 Define *helper*. Who else is described as a Helper in Scripture? (John 14:26)

9 According to Genesis 2, how do Adam and Eve differ? How are they the same?

10 Define *one flesh* from verse 24. What do you learn about Adam and Eve's garden relationship?

11 What did you learn about God this week?

12 Ponder and praise God. Thank Him for the lessons you have learned.

take it to *heart*

SO WHEN THE WOMAN SAW
THAT THE TREE WAS GOOD
FOR FOOD, AND THAT IT WAS A
DELIGHT TO THE EYES, AND THAT
THE TREE WAS TO BE DESIRED
TO MAKE ONE WISE, SHE TOOK
OF ITS FRUIT AND ATE...

GENESIS 3:6

chapter *three*

GENESIS 3

take *note*

NOTES ON GENESIS 3

take *note*

day *one*

GENESIS 3:1-7

READ

[1] Now the serpent was more crafty than any other beast of the field that the Lord God had made.

He said to the woman, "Did God actually say, 'You shall not eat of any tree in the garden'?" [2] And the woman said to the serpent, "We may eat of the fruit of the trees in the garden, [3] but God said, 'You shall not eat of the fruit of the tree that is in the midst of the garden, neither shall you touch it, lest you die.'" [4] But the serpent said to the woman, "You will not surely die. [5] For God knows that when you eat of it your eyes will be opened, and you will be like God, knowing good and evil." [6] So when the woman saw that the tree was good for food, and that it was a delight to the eyes, and that the tree was to be desired to make one wise, she took of its fruit and ate, and she also gave some to her husband who was with her, and he ate. [7] Then the eyes of both were opened, and they knew that they were naked. And they sewed fig leaves together and made themselves loincloths.

OBSERVE

INTERPRET

KEY WORDS	DEFINITIONS	CROSS REFERENCES

MAIN POINT(S)	APPLY

PRAY

day *two*

READ

[8] And they heard the sound of the Lord God walking in the garden in the cool of the day, and the man and his wife hid themselves from the presence of the Lord God among the trees of the garden. [9] But the Lord God called to the man and said to him, "Where are you?" [10] And he said, "I heard the sound of you in the garden, and I was afraid, because I was naked, and I hid myself." [11] He said, "Who told you that you were naked? Have you eaten of the tree of which I commanded you not to eat?" [12] The man said, "The woman whom you gave to be with me, she gave me fruit of the tree, and I ate." [13] Then the Lord God said to the woman, "What is this that you have done?" The woman said, "The serpent deceived me, and I ate."

[14] The Lord God said to the serpent,

"Because you have done this,
    cursed are you above all livestock
    and above all beasts of the field;
on your belly you shall go,
    and dust you shall eat
    all the days of your life.
[15] I will put enmity between you and the woman,
    and between your offspring and her offspring;
he shall bruise your head,
    and you shall bruise his heel."

	OBSERVE	INTERPRET

KEY WORDS	DEFINITIONS	CROSS REFERENCES

MAIN POINT(S)	APPLY

PRAY

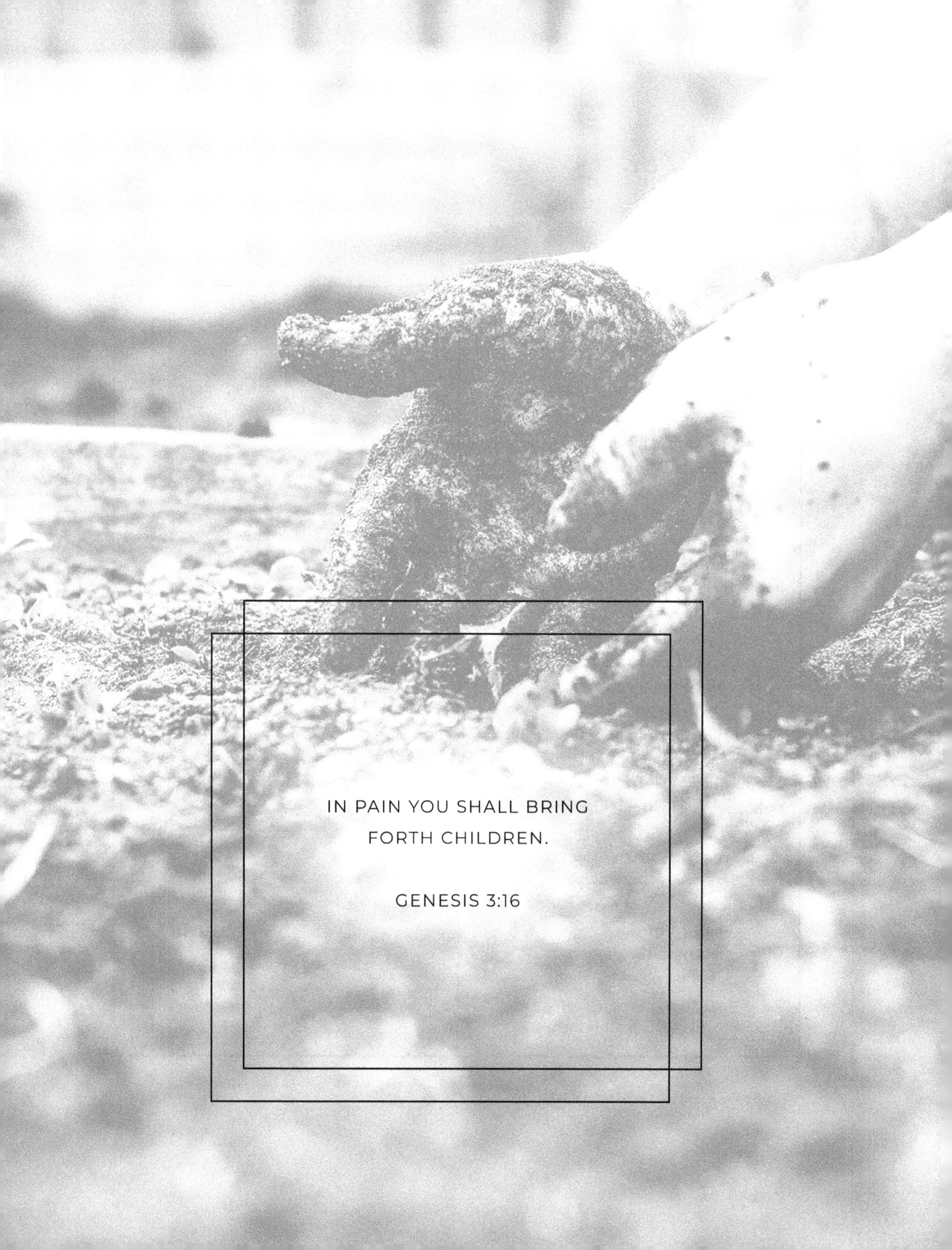
IN PAIN YOU SHALL BRING FORTH CHILDREN.
GENESIS 3:16

day *three*

GENESIS 3:16-19

READ	OBSERVE

¹⁶ To the woman he said,
 	
 "I will surely multiply your pain in childbearing;
    in pain you shall bring forth children.
 Your desire shall be contrary to your husband,
    but he shall rule over you."
 	
 ¹⁷ And to Adam he said,
 	
 "Because you have listened to the voice of your wife
    and have eaten of the tree
 of which I commanded you,
    'You shall not eat of it,'
 cursed is the ground because of you;
    in pain you shall eat of it all the days of your life;
 ¹⁸ thorns and thistles it shall bring forth for you;
    and you shall eat the plants of the field.
 ¹⁹ By the sweat of your face
    you shall eat bread,
 till you return to the ground,
    for out of it you were taken;
 for you are dust,
    and to dust you shall return."	

	INTERPRET

KEY
WORDS

DEFINITIONS

CROSS
REFERENCES

MAIN POINT(S)

APPLY

PRAY

day *four*

GENESIS 3:20-24

READ

20 The man called his wife's name Eve, because she was the mother of all living. 21 And the Lord God made for Adam and for his wife garments of skins and clothed them.

22 Then the Lord God said, "Behold, the man has become like one of us in knowing good and evil. Now, lest he reach out his hand and take also of the tree of life and eat, and live forever—" 23 therefore the Lord God sent him out from the garden of Eden to work the ground from which he was taken. 24 He drove out the man, and at the east of the garden of Eden he placed the cherubim and a flaming sword that turned every way to guard the way to the tree of life.

OBSERVE

INTERPRET

KEY WORDS	DEFINITIONS	CROSS REFERENCES

MAIN POINT(S)	APPLY

PRAY

day *five*

GENESIS 3 | REVIEW AND DISCUSSION QUESTIONS

1 Summarize this week's passage.	2 Write out your favorite verse, perhaps in your own words.
3 Describe the serpent and his lies.	4 What did you learn about Eve?
5 What did you learn about Adam?	6 Define *offspring* in verse 15. Connect to Jesus.

7 Why did Eve eat the fruit? Why did Adam? Who bears guilt?

8 What are the consequences for Eve? For Adam? (v.16-9; 22-23)

9 We are easily deceived. Ask God to reveal a lie that you believe. Confess.

10 Explain how God deals with Adam and Eve after they sin (v.20). How does this apply to you today?

11 What did you learn about God and His grace this week?

12 Ponder and praise God. Thank Him for the lessons you have learned.

take it to *heart*

USE THIS SPACE TO WRITE OUT OR JOURNAL A FAVORITE
VERSE OR PASSAGE FROM THIS WEEK'S STUDY

NOW ADAM KNEW EVE
HIS WIFE, AND SHE
CONCEIVED AND BORE
CAIN, SAYING, "I HAVE
GOTTEN A MAN WITH THE
HELP OF THE LORD."

GENESIS 4:1

chapter *four*

GENESIS 4 & 5

take *note*

NOTES ON GENESIS 4 & 5

take *note*

NOTES ON GENESIS 4 & 5

day *one*

READ

[1] Now Adam knew Eve his wife, and she conceived and bore Cain, saying, "I have gotten a man with the help of the Lord." [2] And again, she bore his brother Abel. Now Abel was a keeper of sheep, and Cain a worker of the ground. [3] In the course of time Cain brought to the Lord an offering of the fruit of the ground, [4] and Abel also brought of the firstborn of his flock and of their fat portions. And the Lord had regard for Abel and his offering, [5] but for Cain and his offering he had no regard. So Cain was very angry, and his face fell. [6] The Lord said to Cain, "Why are you angry, and why has your face fallen? [7] If you do well, will you not be accepted? And if you do not do well, sin is crouching at the door. Its desire is contrary to you, but you must rule over it."

OBSERVE

INTERPRET

KEY WORDS	DEFINITIONS	CROSS REFERENCES

MAIN POINT(S)	APPLY

PRAY

day *two*

READ

⁸ Cain spoke to Abel his brother. And when they were in the field, Cain rose up against his brother Abel and killed him. ⁹ Then the Lord said to Cain, "Where is Abel your brother?" He said, "I do not know; am I my brother's keeper?" ¹⁰ And the Lord said, "What have you done? The voice of your brother's blood is crying to me from the ground. ¹¹ And now you are cursed from the ground, which has opened its mouth to receive your brother's blood from your hand. ¹² When you work the ground, it shall no longer yield to you its strength. You shall be a fugitive and a wanderer on the earth." ¹³ Cain said to the Lord, "My punishment is greater than I can bear. ¹⁴ Behold, you have driven me today away from the ground, and from your face I shall be hidden. I shall be a fugitive and a wanderer on the earth, and whoever finds me will kill me." ¹⁵ Then the Lord said to him, "Not so! If anyone kills Cain, vengeance shall be taken on him sevenfold." And the Lord put a mark on Cain, lest any who found him should attack him. ¹⁶ Then Cain went away from the presence of the Lord and settled in the land of Nod, east of Eden.

OBSERVE

INTERPRET

KEY WORDS	DEFINITIONS	CROSS REFERENCES

MAIN POINT(S)	APPLY

PRAY

day *three*

READ

¹⁷ Cain knew his wife, and she conceived and bore Enoch. When he built a city, he called the name of the city after the name of his son, Enoch. ¹⁸ To Enoch was born Irad, and Irad fathered Mehujael, and Mehujael fathered Methushael, and Methushael fathered Lamech. ¹⁹ And Lamech took two wives. The name of the one was Adah, and the name of the other Zillah. ²⁰ Adah bore Jabal; he was the father of those who dwell in tents and have livestock. ²¹ His brother's name was Jubal; he was the father of all those who play the lyre and pipe. ²² Zillah also bore Tubal-cain; he was the forger of all instruments of bronze and iron. The sister of Tubal-cain was Naamah.

²³ Lamech said to his wives:

"Adah and Zillah, hear my voice;
    you wives of Lamech, listen to what I say:
I have killed a man for wounding me,
    a young man for striking me.
²⁴ If Cain's revenge is sevenfold,
    then Lamech's is seventy-sevenfold."

²⁵ And Adam knew his wife again, and she bore a son and called his name Seth, for she said, "God has appointed for me another offspring instead of Abel, for Cain killed him." ²⁶ To Seth also a son was born, and he called his name Enosh. At that time people began to call upon the name of the Lord.

	OBSERVE	INTERPRET

KEY WORDS	DEFINITIONS	CROSS REFERENCES

MAIN POINT(S)	APPLY

PRAY

AT THAT TIME
PEOPLE BEGAN TO CALL UPON
THE NAME OF THE LORD.

GENESIS 4:26

day *four*

READ

¹ This is the book of the generations of Adam. When God created man, he made him in the likeness of God. ² Male and female he created them, and he blessed them and named them Man when they were created. ³ When Adam had lived 130 years, he fathered a son in his own likeness, after his image, and named him Seth. ⁴ The days of Adam after he fathered Seth were 800 years; and he had other sons and daughters. ⁵ Thus all the days that Adam lived were 930 years, and he died.

⁶ When Seth had lived 105 years, he fathered Enosh. ⁷ Seth lived after he fathered Enosh 807 years and had other sons and daughters. ⁸ Thus all the days of Seth were 912 years, and he died.

⁹ When Enosh had lived 90 years, he fathered Kenan. ¹⁰ Enosh lived after he fathered Kenan 815 years and had other sons and daughters. ¹¹ Thus all the days of Enosh were 905 years, and he died.

¹² When Kenan had lived 70 years, he fathered Mahalalel. ¹³ Kenan lived after he fathered Mahalalel 840 years and had other sons and daughters. ¹⁴ Thus all the days of Kenan were 910 years, and he died.

¹⁵ When Mahalalel had lived 65 years, he fathered Jared. ¹⁶ Mahalalel lived after he fathered Jared 830 years and had other sons and daughters. ¹⁷ Thus all the days of Mahalalel were 895 years, and he died.

¹⁸ When Jared had lived 162 years, he fathered Enoch. ¹⁹ Jared lived after he fathered Enoch 800 years and had other sons and daughters. ²⁰ Thus all the days of Jared were 962 years, and he died.

²¹ When Enoch had lived 65 years, he fathered Methuselah. ²² Enoch walked with God after he fathered Methuselah 300 years and had other sons and daughters.

23 Thus all the days of Enoch were 365 years.
24 Enoch walked with God, and he was not, for God took him.

25 When Methuselah had lived 187 years, he fathered Lamech. 26 Methuselah lived after he fathered Lamech 782 years and had other sons and daughters. 27 Thus all the days of Methuselah were 969 years, and he died.

28 When Lamech had lived 182 years, he fathered a son 29 and called his name Noah, saying, "Out of the ground that the Lord has cursed, this one shall bring us relief from our work and from the painful toil of our hands." 30 Lamech lived after he fathered Noah 595 years and had other sons and daughters. 31 Thus all the days of Lamech were 777 years, and he died.

32 After Noah was 500 years old, Noah fathered Shem, Ham, and Japheth.

OBSERVE

INTERPRET

KEY WORDS	DEFINITIONS	CROSS REFERENCES

MAIN POINT(S)	APPLY

PRAY

THE MAN CALLED HIS
WIFE'S NAME EVE,
BECAUSE SHE WAS THE
MOTHER OF ALL LIVING.

GENESIS 3:20

day *five*

1 Summarize this week's passage.	2 Write out your favorite verse, perhaps in your own words.
3 What did you learn about Eve and her heart from 4:1-2?	4 How does God demonstrate grace to Eve? Apply.
5 Explain God's grace towards Cain (v.6-7).	6 How else could Cain have responded to God, leading to a different ending? Apply.

7 Ponder the events from Eve's perspective, listing her joys and sorrows.

8 Can you relate to Eve in some way? Explain.

9 What do you learn about Adam and Eve from Genesis 5?

10 List and define the repeated words in Genesis 5.

11 What do you learn about God and man through the genealogy?

12 Ponder and praise God. Thank Him for the lessons you have learned.

take it to *heart*

USE THIS SPACE TO WRITE OUT OR JOURNAL A FAVORITE
VERSE OR PASSAGE FROM THIS WEEK'S STUDY

AND THE ANGEL SAID TO
HER, "DO NOT BE AFRAID,
MARY, FOR YOU HAVE
FOUND FAVOR WITH GOD."

LUKE 1:30

chapter *five*

LUKE 1:1-38

take *note*

NOTES ON LUKE 1:1-38

take *note*

NOTES ON LUKE 1:1-38

day *one*

READ

¹ Inasmuch as many have undertaken to compile a narrative of the things that have been accomplished among us, ² just as those who from the beginning were eyewitnesses and ministers of the word have delivered them to us, ³ it seemed good to me also, having followed all things closely for some time past, to write an orderly account for you, most excellent Theophilus, ⁴ that you may have certainty concerning the things you have been taught.

⁵ In the days of Herod, king of Judea, there was a priest named Zechariah, of the division of Abijah. And he had a wife from the daughters of Aaron, and her name was Elizabeth. ⁶ And they were both righteous before God, walking blamelessly in all the commandments and statutes of the Lord. ⁷ But they had no child, because Elizabeth was barren, and both were advanced in years.

OBSERVE

INTERPRET

KEY WORDS	DEFINITIONS	CROSS REFERENCES

MAIN POINT(S)	APPLY

PRAY

day *two*

READ

8 Now while he was serving as priest before God when his division was on duty, 9 according to the custom of the priesthood, he was chosen by lot to enter the temple of the Lord and burn incense. 10 And the whole multitude of the people were praying outside at the hour of incense. 11 And there appeared to him an angel of the Lord standing on the right side of the altar of incense. 12 And Zechariah was troubled when he saw him, and fear fell upon him. 13 But the angel said to him, "Do not be afraid, Zechariah, for your prayer has been heard, and your wife Elizabeth will bear you a son, and you shall call his name John. 14 And you will have joy and gladness, and many will rejoice at his birth, 15 for he will be great before the Lord. And he must not drink wine or strong drink, and he will be filled with the Holy Spirit, even from his mother's womb. 16 And he will turn many of the children of Israel to the Lord their God,

17 and he will go before him in the spirit and power of Elijah, to turn the hearts of the fathers to the children, and the disobedient to the wisdom of the just, to make ready for the Lord a people prepared."

18 And Zechariah said to the angel, "How shall I know this? For I am an old man, and my wife is advanced in years." 19 And the angel answered him, "I am Gabriel. I stand in the presence of God, and I was sent to speak to you and to bring you this good news. 20 And behold, you will be silent and unable to speak until the day that these things take place, because you did not believe my words, which will be fulfilled in their time." 21 And the people were waiting for Zechariah, and they were wondering at his delay in the temple. 22 And when he came out, he was unable to speak to them, and they realized that he had seen a vision in the temple. And he kept making signs to them and remained mute. 23 And when his time of service was ended, he went to his home.

24 After these days his wife Elizabeth conceived, and for five months she kept herself hidden, saying, 25 "Thus the Lord has done for me in the days when he looked on me, to take away my reproach among people."

	OBSERVE	INTERPRET

KEY WORDS	DEFINITIONS	CROSS REFERENCES

MAIN POINT(S)	APPLY

PRAY

AND BEHOLD, YOU WILL
CONCEIVE IN YOUR
WOMB AND BEAR A SON,
AND YOU SHALL CALL
HIS NAME JESUS.

LUKE 1:31

day *three*

LUKE 1:26-33

READ

²⁶ In the sixth month the angel Gabriel was sent from God to a city of Galilee named Nazareth, ²⁷ to a virgin betrothed to a man whose name was Joseph, of the house of David. And the virgin's name was Mary. ²⁸ And he came to her and said, "Greetings, O favored one, the Lord is with you!" ²⁹ But she was greatly troubled at the saying, and tried to discern what sort of greeting this might be. ³⁰ And the angel said to her, "Do not be afraid, Mary, for you have found favor with God. ³¹ And behold, you will conceive in your womb and bear a son, and you shall call his name Jesus. ³² He will be great and will be called the Son of the Most High. And the Lord God will give to him the throne of his father David, ³³ and he will reign over the house of Jacob forever, and of his kingdom there will be no end."

OBSERVE

INTERPRET

KEY WORDS	DEFINITIONS	CROSS REFERENCES

MAIN POINT(S)	APPLY

PRAY

day *four*

READ	OBSERVE	INTERPRET
34 And Mary said to the angel, "How will this be, since I am a virgin?" 35 And the angel answered her, "The Holy Spirit will come upon you, and the power of the Most High will overshadow you; therefore the child to be born will be called holy—the Son of God. 36 And behold, your relative Elizabeth in her old age has also conceived a son, and this is the sixth month with her who was called barren. 37 For nothing will be impossible with God." 38 And Mary said, "Behold, I am the servant of the Lord; let it be to me according to your word." And the angel departed from her.		

KEY WORDS	DEFINITIONS	CROSS REFERENCES

MAIN POINT(S)	APPLY

PRAY

day *five*

LUKE 1:1-38 | REVIEW AND DISCUSSION QUESTIONS

1 Summarize this week's passage.	2 Write out your favorite verse, perhaps in your own words.
3 What did you learn about Luke, the author of this narrative? Can we trust his words? Why?	4 Who are Zechariah and Elizabeth? What do you learn about them?
5 What sin is behind Zechariah's question to Gabriel? (v.20) Apply.	6 Are there promises in God's Word that you struggle to believe?

7 Who is Gabriel, and what do you learn about God from him?

8 Describe Mary's response to the angel. Consider how others would receive the news.

9 How does her response apply to you?

10 Ponder and list all you learned about Mary.

11 What did you learn about God and His grace this week?

12 Ponder and praise God. Thank Him for the lessons you have learned.

take it to *heart*

USE THIS SPACE TO WRITE OUT OR JOURNAL A FAVORITE
VERSE OR PASSAGE FROM THIS WEEK'S STUDY

"MY SOUL MAGNIFIES
THE LORD,
AND MY SPIRIT REJOICES
IN GOD MY SAVIOR..."

LUKE 1:46-47

chapter *six*

LUKE 1:39-80

take *note*

NOTES ON LUKE 1:39-80

take *note*

NOTES ON LUKE 1:39-80

day *one*

LUKE 1:39-45

READ	OBSERVE	INTERPRET
³⁹ In those days Mary arose and went with haste into the hill country, to a town in Judah, ⁴⁰ and she entered the house of Zechariah and greeted Elizabeth. ⁴¹ And when Elizabeth heard the greeting of Mary, the baby leaped in her womb. And Elizabeth was filled with the Holy Spirit, ⁴² and she exclaimed with a loud cry, "Blessed are you among women, and blessed is the fruit of your womb! ⁴³ And why is this granted to me that the mother of my Lord should come to me? ⁴⁴ For behold, when the sound of your greeting came to my ears, the baby in my womb leaped for joy. ⁴⁵ And blessed is she who believed that there would be a fulfillment of what was spoken to her from the Lord."		

KEY WORDS	DEFINITIONS	CROSS REFERENCES

MAIN POINT(S)	APPLY

PRAY

day *two*

LUKE 1:46-56

READ

⁴⁶ And Mary said,

"My soul magnifies the Lord,
⁴⁷ and my spirit rejoices in God my Savior,
⁴⁸ for he has looked on the humble estate of his servant.
   For behold, from now on all generations will call me blessed;
⁴⁹ for he who is mighty has done great things for me,
   and holy is his name.
⁵⁰ And his mercy is for those who fear him
   from generation to generation.
⁵¹ He has shown strength with his arm;
   he has scattered the proud in the thoughts of their hearts;
⁵² he has brought down the mighty from their thrones
   and exalted those of humble estate;
⁵³ he has filled the hungry with good things,
   and the rich he has sent away empty.
⁵⁴ He has helped his servant Israel,
   in remembrance of his mercy,
⁵⁵ as he spoke to our fathers,
   to Abraham and to his offspring forever."

⁵⁶ And Mary remained with her about three months and returned to her home.

	OBSERVE	INTERPRET

KEY WORDS	DEFINITIONS	CROSS REFERENCES

MAIN POINT(S)	APPLY

PRAY

"BLESSED BE THE
LORD GOD OF ISRAEL,
FOR HE HAS VISITED
AND REDEEMED
HIS PEOPLE."

LUKE 1:68

day *three*

LUKE 1:57-66

READ

57 Now the time came for Elizabeth to give birth, and she bore a son. 58 And her neighbors and relatives heard that the Lord had shown great mercy to her, and they rejoiced with her. 59 And on the eighth day they came to circumcise the child. And they would have called him Zechariah after his father, 60 but his mother answered, "No; he shall be called John." 61 And they said to her, "None of your relatives is called by this name." 62 And they made signs to his father, inquiring what he wanted him to be called. 63 And he asked for a writing tablet and wrote, "His name is John." And they all wondered. 64 And immediately his mouth was opened and his tongue loosed, and he spoke, blessing God. 65 And fear came on all their neighbors. And all these things were talked about through all the hill country of Judea, 66 and all who heard them laid them up in their hearts, saying, "What then will this child be?" For the hand of the Lord was with him.

OBSERVE

INTERPRET

KEY WORDS	DEFINITIONS	CROSS REFERENCES

MAIN POINT(S)	APPLY

PRAY

day *four*

LUKE 1:67-80

READ

⁶⁷ And his father Zechariah was filled with the Holy Spirit and prophesied, saying,

⁶⁸ "Blessed be the Lord God of Israel,
    for he has visited and redeemed his people
⁶⁹ and has raised up a horn of salvation for us
    in the house of his servant David,
⁷⁰ as he spoke by the mouth of his holy prophets from of old,
⁷¹ that we should be saved from our enemies
    and from the hand of all who hate us;
⁷² to show the mercy promised to our fathers
    and to remember his holy covenant,
⁷³ the oath that he swore to our father Abraham, to grant us
⁷⁴ that we, being delivered from the hand of our enemies,
might serve him without fear,
⁷⁵ in holiness and righteousness before him all our days.
⁷⁶ And you, child, will be called the prophet of the Most High;
    for you will go before the Lord to prepare his ways,
⁷⁷ to give knowledge of salvation to his people
    in the forgiveness of their sins,
⁷⁸ because of the tender mercy of our God,
    whereby the sunrise shall visit us from on high
⁷⁹ to give light to those who sit in darkness and in the shadow of death,
    to guide our feet into the way of peace."

⁸⁰ And the child grew and became strong in spirit, and he was in the wilderness until the day of his public appearance to Israel.

	OBSERVE	INTERPRET

KEY WORDS	DEFINITIONS	CROSS REFERENCES

MAIN POINT(S)	APPLY

PRAY

"AND [HE] HAS RAISED
UP A HORN OF
SALVATION FOR US
IN THE HOUSE OF HIS
SERVANT DAVID."

LUKE 1:69

day *five*

1 Summarize this week's passage.	2 Write out your favorite verse, perhaps in your own words.
3 Why do you think Mary went to visit Elizabeth?	4 What do you learn about Elizabeth? What do you learn about the babies Mary and Elizabeth carry?
5 How would Mary be encouraged? Was she? Use Scripture to back up your answer.	6 What do you learn about Mary from her song recorded by Luke? (v.46-55)

7 Describe what happens with Zechariah at the circumcision of John the Baptist.

8 How would Mary hear about these things? How would she feel? (v.65-66)

9 What do you learn from Zechariah's prophecy?

10 What did you learn about Mary? How would you describe her?

11 What did you learn about God and His grace this week?

12 Ponder and praise God. Thank Him for the lessons you have learned.

take it to *heart*

USE THIS SPACE TO WRITE OUT OR JOURNAL A FAVORITE
VERSE OR PASSAGE FROM THIS WEEK'S STUDY

BUT MARY
TREASURED UP
ALL THESE THINGS,
PONDERING THEM
IN HER HEART.

LUKE 2:19

chapter *seven*

LUKE 2

take *note*

NOTES ON LUKE 2

take *note*

NOTES ON LUKE 2

day *one*

LUKE 2:1-7

READ	OBSERVE	INTERPRET
[1] In those days a decree went out from Caesar Augustus that all the world should be registered. [2] This was the first registration when Quirinius was governor of Syria. [3] And all went to be registered, each to his own town. [4] And Joseph also went up from Galilee, from the town of Nazareth, to Judea, to the city of David, which is called Bethlehem, because he was of the house and lineage of David, [5] to be registered with Mary, his betrothed, who was with child. [6] And while they were there, the time came for her to give birth. [7] And she gave birth to her firstborn son and wrapped him in swaddling cloths and laid him in a manger, because there was no place for them in the inn.		

KEY WORDS	DEFINITIONS	CROSS REFERENCES

MAIN POINT(S)	APPLY

PRAY

day *two*

READ

⁸ And in the same region there were shepherds out in the field, keeping watch over their flock by night. ⁹ And an angel of the Lord appeared to them, and the glory of the Lord shone around them, and they were filled with great fear. ¹⁰ And the angel said to them, "Fear not, for behold, I bring you good news of great joy that will be for all the people. ¹¹ For unto you is born this day in the city of David a Savior, who is Christ the Lord. ¹² And this will be a sign for you: you will find a baby wrapped in swaddling cloths and lying in a manger." ¹³ And suddenly there was with the angel a multitude of the heavenly host praising God and saying,

¹⁴ "Glory to God in the highest,
   and on earth peace among those with whom he is pleased!"

¹⁵ When the angels went away from them into heaven, the shepherds said to one another, "Let us go over to Bethlehem and see this thing that has happened, which the Lord has made known to us." ¹⁶ And they went with haste and found Mary and Joseph, and the baby lying in a manger. ¹⁷ And when they saw it, they made known the saying that had been told them concerning this child. ¹⁸ And all who heard it wondered at what the shepherds told them. ¹⁹ But Mary treasured up all these things, pondering them in her heart. ²⁰ And the shepherds returned, glorifying and praising God for all they had heard and seen, as it had been told them.

²¹ And at the end of eight days, when he was circumcised, he was called Jesus, the name given by the angel before he was conceived in the womb.

	OBSERVE	INTERPRET

KEY WORDS	DEFINITIONS	CROSS REFERENCES

MAIN POINT(S)	APPLY

PRAY

AND SHE GAVE BIRTH
TO HER FIRSTBORN SON
AND WRAPPED HIM IN
SWADDLING CLOTHS AND
LAID HIM IN A MANGER,
BECAUSE THERE WAS NO
PLACE FOR THEM IN THE INN.

LUKE 2:7

day *three*

LUKE 2:22-40

22 And when the time came for their purification according to the Law of Moses, they brought him up to Jerusalem to present him to the Lord 23 (as it is written in the Law of the Lord, "Every male who first opens the womb shall be called holy to the Lord") 24 and to offer a sacrifice according to what is said in the Law of the Lord, "a pair of turtledoves, or two young pigeons." 25 Now there was a man in Jerusalem, whose name was Simeon, and this man was righteous and devout, waiting for the consolation of Israel, and the Holy Spirit was upon him. 26 And it had been revealed to him by the Holy Spirit that he would not see death before he had seen the Lord's Christ. 27 And he came in the Spirit into the temple, and when the parents brought in the child Jesus, to do for him according to the custom of the Law, 28 he took him up in his arms and blessed God and said,

29 "Lord, now you are letting your servant depart in peace,
    according to your word;
30 for my eyes have seen your salvation
31 that you have prepared in the presence of all peoples,
32 a light for revelation to the Gentiles,
    and for glory to your people Israel."

33 And his father and his mother marveled at what was said about him. 34 And Simeon blessed them and said to Mary his mother, "Behold, this child is appointed for the fall and rising of many in Israel, and for a sign that is opposed 35 (and a sword will pierce through your own soul also), so that thoughts from many hearts may be revealed."

36 And there was a prophetess, Anna, the daughter of Phanuel, of the tribe of Asher. She was advanced in years, having lived with her husband seven years from when she was a virgin, 37 and then as a widow until she was eighty-four. She did not depart from the temple, worshiping with fasting and prayer night and day. 38 And

coming up at that very hour she began to give thanks to God and to speak of him to all who were waiting for the redemption of Jerusalem.

[39] And when they had performed everything according to the Law of the Lord, they returned into Galilee, to their own town of Nazareth. [40] And the child grew and became strong, filled with wisdom. And the favor of God was upon him.

OBSERVE	INTERPRET

KEY WORDS	DEFINITIONS	CROSS REFERENCES

MAIN POINT(S)	APPLY

PRAY

AND HIS FATHER
AND HIS MOTHER
MARVELED AT WHAT
WAS SAID ABOUT HIM.

LUKE 2:33

day *four*

READ

⁴¹ Now his parents went to Jerusalem every year at the Feast of the Passover. ⁴² And when he was twelve years old, they went up according to custom. ⁴³ And when the feast was ended, as they were returning, the boy Jesus stayed behind in Jerusalem. His parents did not know it, ⁴⁴ but supposing him to be in the group they went a day's journey, but then they began to search for him among their relatives and acquaintances, ⁴⁵ and when they did not find him, they returned to Jerusalem, searching for him. ⁴⁶ After three days they found him in the temple, sitting among the teachers, listening to them and asking them questions. ⁴⁷ And all who heard him were amazed at his understanding and his answers. ⁴⁸ And when his parents saw him, they were astonished. And his mother said to him, "Son, why have you treated us so? Behold, your father and I have been searching for you in great distress." ⁴⁹ And he said to them, "Why were you looking for me? Did you not know that I must be in my Father's house?" ⁵⁰ And they did not understand the saying that he spoke to them. ⁵¹ And he went down with them and came to Nazareth and was submissive to them. And his mother treasured up all these things in her heart.

⁵² And Jesus increased in wisdom and in stature and in favor with God and man.

	OBSERVE	INTERPRET

KEY WORDS	DEFINITIONS	CROSS REFERENCES

MAIN POINT(S)	APPLY

PRAY

AND JESUS INCREASED
IN WISDOM AND IN
STATURE AND IN FAVOR
WITH GOD AND MAN.

LUKE 2:52

day *five*

1 Summarize this week's passage.	2 Write out your favorite verse, perhaps in your own words.
3 Where did Mary give birth to her baby, and why? How might this have felt?	4 What can you learn about Jesus from the shepherds' encounter with the angels? How do the shepherds react?
5 How would Mary be encouraged by them? Use Scripture to back up your answer.	6 Describe Mary and Joseph's encounter with Simeon and Anna at the temple. What do you learn about Jesus?

7 Again, how would Mary be encouraged? How do you know she was encouraged?

8 In v.41-52, how long was Jesus missing? How might Mary have felt?

9 What does the phrase "treasured up all these things in her heart" mean?

10 How does this chapter relate to Eve?

11 What did you learn about God and His grace this week?

12 Ponder and praise God. Thank Him for the lessons you have learned.

take it to *heart*

USE THIS SPACE TO WRITE OUT OR JOURNAL A FAVORITE
VERSE OR PASSAGE FROM THIS WEEK'S STUDY

SHE WILL BEAR A SON,
AND YOU SHALL CALL
HIS NAME JESUS, FOR HE
WILL SAVE HIS PEOPLE
FROM THEIR SINS.

MATTHEW 1:21

chapter *eight*

OTHER PASSAGES WITH MARY

take *note*

NOTES ON OTHER PASSAGES WITH MARY

take *note*

NOTES ON OTHER PASSAGES WITH MARY

day *one*

MATTHEW 1:18-25

READ	OBSERVE
[18] Now the birth of Jesus Christ took place in this way. When his mother Mary had been betrothed to Joseph, before they came together she was found to be with child from the Holy Spirit. [19] And her husband Joseph, being a just man and unwilling to put her to shame, resolved to divorce her quietly. [20] But as he considered these things, behold, an angel of the Lord appeared to him in a dream, saying, "Joseph, son of David, do not fear to take Mary as your wife, for that which is conceived in her is from the Holy Spirit. [21] She will bear a son, and you shall call his name Jesus, for he will save his people from their sins." [22] All this took place to fulfill what the Lord had spoken by the prophet:	
[23] "Behold, the virgin shall conceive and bear a son, and they shall call his name Immanuel"	**INTERPRET**
(which means, God with us). [24] When Joseph woke from sleep, he did as the angel of the Lord commanded him: he took his wife, [25] but knew her not until she had given birth to a son. And he called his name Jesus.	

KEY WORDS	DEFINITIONS	CROSS REFERENCES

MAIN POINT(S)	APPLY

PRAY

day *two*

READ

¹ Now after Jesus was born in Bethlehem of Judea in the days of Herod the king, behold, wise men from the east came to Jerusalem, ² saying, "Where is he who has been born king of the Jews? For we saw his star when it rose and have come to worship him." ³ When Herod the king heard this, he was troubled, and all Jerusalem with him; ⁴ and assembling all the chief priests and scribes of the people, he inquired of them where the Christ was to be born. ⁵ They told him, "In Bethlehem of Judea, for so it is written by the prophet:

⁶ "'And you, O Bethlehem, in the land of Judah,
    are by no means least among the rulers of Judah;
for from you shall come a ruler
    who will shepherd my people Israel.'"

⁷ Then Herod summoned the wise men secretly and ascertained from them what time the star had appeared. ⁸ And he sent them to Bethlehem, saying, "Go and search diligently for the child, and when you have found him, bring me word, that I too may come and worship him." ⁹ After listening to the king, they went on their way. And behold, the star that they had seen when it rose went before them until it came to rest over the place where the child was. ¹⁰ When they saw the star, they rejoiced exceedingly with great joy. ¹¹ And going into the house, they saw the child with Mary his mother, and they fell down and worshiped him. Then, opening their treasures, they offered him gifts, gold and frankincense and myrrh. ¹² And being warned in a dream not to return to Herod, they departed to their own country by another way.

	OBSERVE	INTERPRET

KEY WORDS	DEFINITIONS	CROSS REFERENCES

MAIN POINT(S)	APPLY

PRAY

"WHERE IS HE WHO
HAS BEEN BORN KING
OF THE JEWS? FOR WE
SAW HIS STAR WHEN IT
ROSE AND HAVE COME
TO WORSHIP HIM."

MATTHEW 2:2

day *three*

MATTHEW 2:13-23

READ

¹³ Now when they had departed, behold, an angel of the Lord appeared to Joseph in a dream and said, "Rise, take the child and his mother, and flee to Egypt, and remain there until I tell you, for Herod is about to search for the child, to destroy him." ¹⁴ And he rose and took the child and his mother by night and departed to Egypt ¹⁵ and remained there until the death of Herod. This was to fulfill what the Lord had spoken by the prophet, "Out of Egypt I called my son."

¹⁶ Then Herod, when he saw that he had been tricked by the wise men, became furious, and he sent and killed all the male children in Bethlehem and in all that region who were two years old or under, according to the time that he had ascertained from the wise men. ¹⁷ Then was fulfilled what was spoken by the prophet Jeremiah:

¹⁸ "A voice was heard in Ramah,
    weeping and loud lamentation,
Rachel weeping for her children;
    she refused to be comforted, because they are no more."

¹⁹ But when Herod died, behold, an angel of the Lord appeared in a dream to Joseph in Egypt, ²⁰ saying, "Rise, take the child and his mother and go to the land of Israel, for those who sought the child's life are dead." ²¹ And he rose and took the child and his mother and went to the land of Israel. ²² But when he heard that Archelaus was reigning over Judea in place of his father Herod, he was afraid to go there, and being warned in a dream he withdrew to the district of Galilee. ²³ And he went and lived in a city called Nazareth, so that what was spoken by the prophets might be fulfilled, that he would be called a Nazarene.

	OBSERVE	INTERPRET

KEY WORDS	DEFINITIONS	CROSS REFERENCES

MAIN POINT(S)	APPLY

PRAY

"RISE, TAKE THE CHILD AND HIS MOTHER, AND FLEE TO EGYPT, AND REMAIN THERE UNTIL I TELL YOU, FOR HEROD IS ABOUT TO SEARCH FOR THE CHILD, TO DESTROY HIM."

MATTHEW 2:13

day *four*

JOHN 2:1-12 | JOHN 19:25-27 | ACTS 1:14

READ

¹ On the third day there was a wedding at Cana in Galilee, and the mother of Jesus was there. ² Jesus also was invited to the wedding with his disciples. ³ When the wine ran out, the mother of Jesus said to him, "They have no wine." ⁴ And Jesus said to her, "Woman, what does this have to do with me? My hour has not yet come." ⁵ His mother said to the servants, "Do whatever he tells you."

⁶ Now there were six stone water jars there for the Jewish rites of purification, each holding twenty or thirty gallons. ⁷ Jesus said to the servants, "Fill the jars with water." And they filled them up to the brim. ⁸ And he said to them, "Now draw some out and take it to the master of the feast." So they took it. ⁹ When the master of the feast tasted the water now become wine, and did not know where it came from (though the servants who had drawn the water knew), the master of the feast called the bridegroom ¹⁰ and said to him, "Everyone serves the good wine first, and when people have drunk freely, then the poor wine. But you have kept the good wine until now." ¹¹ This, the first of his signs, Jesus did at Cana in Galilee, and manifested his glory. And his disciples believed in him.

¹² After this he went down to Capernaum, with his mother and his brothers and his disciples, and they stayed there for a few days.

---

²⁵ but standing by the cross of Jesus were his mother and his mother's sister, Mary the wife of Clopas, and Mary Magdalene. ²⁶ When Jesus saw his mother and the disciple whom he loved standing nearby, he said to his mother, "Woman, behold, your son!" ²⁷ Then he said to the disciple, "Behold, your mother!" And from that hour the disciple took her to his own home.

---

¹⁴ All these with one accord were devoting themselves to prayer, together with the women and Mary the mother of Jesus, and his brothers.

	OBSERVE	INTERPRET

KEY WORDS	DEFINITIONS	CROSS REFERENCES

MAIN POINT(S)	APPLY

PRAY

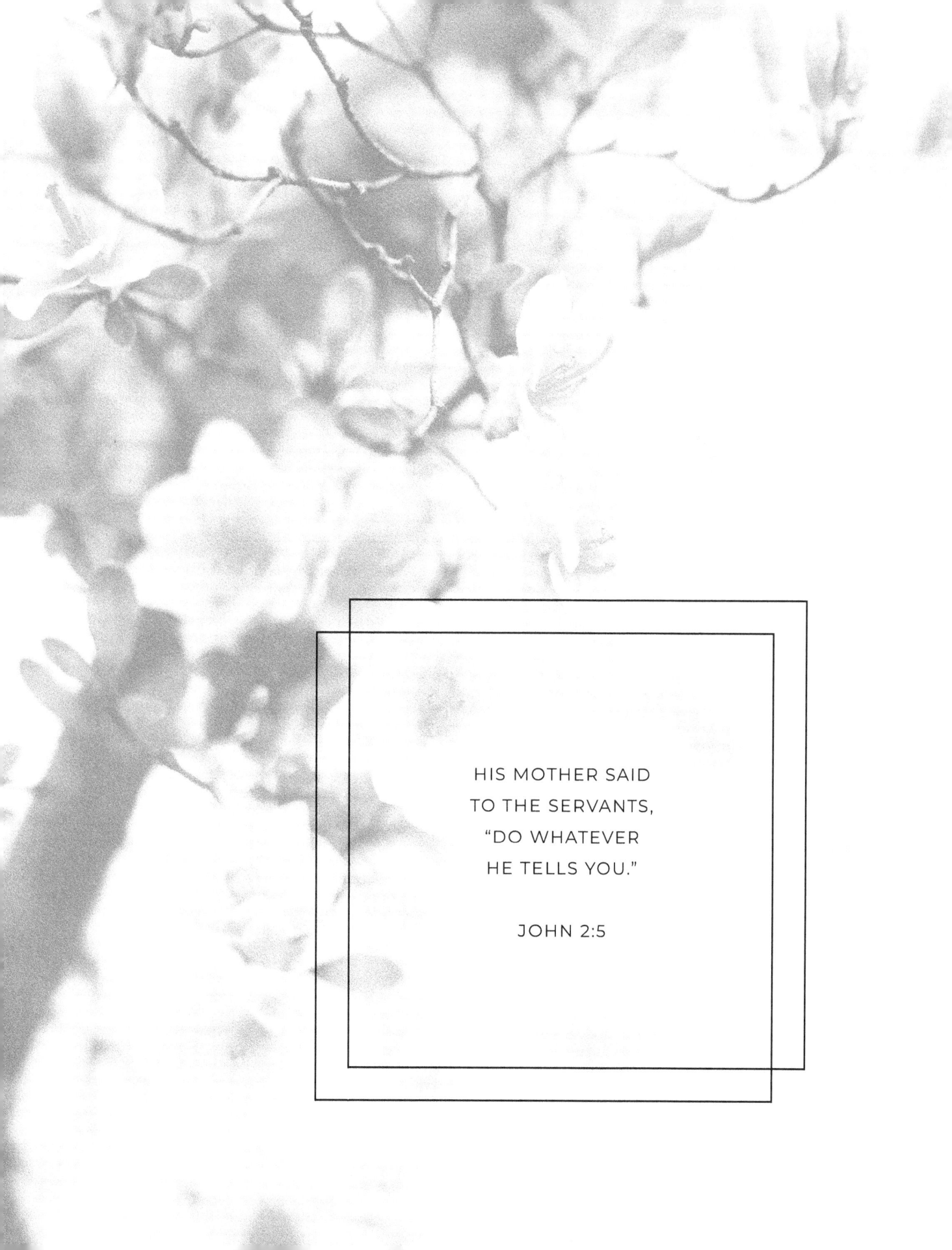

HIS MOTHER SAID
TO THE SERVANTS,
"DO WHATEVER
HE TELLS YOU."

JOHN 2:5

day *five*

1 Summarize this week's passages.	2 Write out your favorite verse, perhaps in your own words.
3 How did others (including Joseph) perceive Mary? What did Mary endure to carry the Son of God?	4 What do you learn about Jesus from the angel that visits Joseph?
5 What do the wise men teach us about Jesus? How might this have inspired Mary?	6 Describe the flight to Egypt and the death of all male babies in Bethlehem from Mary's perspective.

7 Describe John's account of the wedding in Cana from Mary's perspective. (John 2:1-12)

8 Read John 19:25-27. What kind of pain did Mary experience in childbearing?

9 Read Acts 1:14. What do you learn about Mary?

10 Describe Mary's pain and hope in bearing the Savior of the World. How does this relate to Eve's pain and hope?

11 What did you learn about God and His grace this week?

12 Ponder and praise God. Thank Him for the lessons you have learned.

take it to *heart*

USE THIS SPACE TO WRITE OUT OR JOURNAL A FAVORITE
VERSE OR PASSAGE FROM THIS WEEK'S STUDY

"...HE WHO IS MIGHTY HAS
DONE GREAT THINGS FOR ME,
AND HOLY IS HIS NAME."

LUKE 1:49

final *thoughts*

WRAPPING UP | A COMPARISON OF EVE & MARY

review *eve*

RE-READ THE PASSAGES: *Genesis 1-5. Review and ponder what you have learned about Eve.*

1 Create a brief chronological outline of her life.	2 Share your favorite verse about Eve and explain.
3 What were Eve's outstanding qualities? Apply.	4 Share Eve's weaknesses. Is there a warning or confession to apply?
5 Can you identify Eve's joys and sorrows?	6 What did you learn about Jesus through studying Eve? Explain how Genesis 3:15 points to Him.

7 How will you remember Eve after this study?

8 Is there one word that could describe Eve's life?

9 How does God view Eve? (Use Scripture.)

10 What do you learn about God through His interactions with Eve?

11 Apply this to your own life.

12 How can we look at Eve, others, and ourselves with grace and truth?

review *mary*

1 Create a brief chronological outline of Mary's life.	2 Share your favorite verse about Mary and explain.
3 What were Mary's outstanding qualities? Apply.	4 Share any weakness you noticed in Mary. Is there a warning to apply?
5 Can you identify Mary's joys and sorrows?	6 How would you like to emulate Mary's life?

7 How will you remember Mary? Is there one word that could describe her?

8 What did you learn about Jesus through studying Mary?

9 How does God view Mary? (Use Scripture.)

10 What do you learn about God from His interactions with Mary?

11 Apply this to your own life.

12 Praise God for what you learned about Him.

final *thoughts*

WRAPPING UP | SEEING JESUS THROUGH EVE & MARY

1 Summarize Eve's story and her connection to Jesus.	2 How does God view Eve? Explain using Scripture.
3 Do you find Eve relatable? Explain.	4 Summarize Mary's story and her connection to Jesus.
5 How does God view Mary? Explain using Scripture.	6 What do you admire about Mary?

7 List the similarities between Eve & Mary.

8 How do these women pave the way for the good news of Jesus?

9 How is Jesus the ultimate life-giver?

10 What did you learn about God through studying Eve and Mary?

11 How would you summarize this study in one sentence? Could you summarize using only one word?

12 How has God transformed your heart through this study? How will you live or think differently? Praise and thank Him.

take it to *heart*

take *note*

NOTES ON COMPARING EVE & MARY

take *note*

NOTES ON COMPARING EVE & MARY

leader *guide*

MAXIMIZING THE SMALL-GROUP EXPERIENCE

GO THEREFORE AND MAKE
DISCIPLES OF ALL NATIONS,
BAPTIZING THEM IN THE
NAME OF THE FATHER AND
OF THE SON AND OF THE
HOLY SPIRIT, TEACHING THEM
TO OBSERVE ALL THAT I HAVE
COMMANDED YOU.

MATTHEW 28:19-20

introduction

LEADING WOMEN THROUGH **SIMPLY BIBLE**

Welcome to SIMPLY BIBLE! Thank you for your commitment to walk alongside others for this season of exploring God's Word. In my own life, God has proven Himself faithful. Time and again as I step out in faith to lead and seek to be a blessing to others, the blessing seems to always be mine. He is gracious that way. So, it is my heartfelt prayer for leaders that as you seek to be a blessing, you, too, will be blessed beyond measure by the experience of shepherding others through God's Word. Truly, what a privilege to facilitate conversations that point to Christ!

The primary objective of SIMPLY BIBLE is this:

> To inspire us to love God with all our
> heart, soul, mind, and strength, and to
> love others as ourselves.
>
> LUKE 10:27

And you, the small-group leader, will play an important role in inspiring Bible students to do exactly that! You will lead your group through meaningful conversations, with the help of the discussion questions found at the end of every chapter in this workbook. The intent is to help others grow and connect with Jesus and with one another, gently guiding them to authentic relationships with Jesus and one another.

Because our goal for study is to see others growing in relationship with Christ and one another, you do not need to be a Bible expert to lead discussions about His Word. You only need a heart to love and encourage. So what does effective small-group leadership look like?

GUARDING YOUR HEART

Ethos is a Latin word that denotes the fundamental character or spirit of a community, group, or person. When used to discuss dramatic literature, ethos is the moral element that determines a character's action rather than his or her thought or emotion. [1] Ethos points to the inward being, to the moral fabric of the heart. In biblical language, ethos absolutely relates to a person's heart. And our ethos, our heart, is important to God.

His Word tells us:

> Above all else, guard your heart, for
> everything you do flows from it.
>
> **PROVERBS 4:23 (NIV)**

Above *all* else, guard your heart. Why? Because *everything* we do flows from the heart, from our inward being. And that *everything* includes leading others through God's Word. If we want to see men and women growing in authentic relationships with Christ and with one another, that process must first begin in our own hearts.

> For the Lord sees not as man sees:
> man looks on the outward appearance,
> but the Lord looks on the heart.
>
> **I SAMUEL 16:7**

---

[1] **ethos**. Dictionary.com. *Dictionary.com Unabridged.* Random House, Inc. http://www.dictionary.com/browse/observe (accessed: March 16, 2018).

So often, as individuals and as ministry groups, we get caught up in appearances. I'm guilty. How easy is it for us as leaders to dress ourselves for Bible study, look nice on the outside, make the tables look inviting, share a few pleasant words, fill in the blank spaces of our studies, and all the while, never touch the core of our hearts? God looks at the heart. Perhaps we should, too.

Truly, there is much to share concerning effectively "guarding our hearts" while leading others in inductive Bible study. However, for our purposes today, let's keep things simple and limit our necessary ingredients to three.

1. Jesus
2. Prayer
3. The Word

By guarding our hearts in these ways, successful Bible study leadership is certain. Let's briefly consider each.

GUARDING YOUR HEART WITH **JESUS.**

This may seem so obvious, even "in your face," but honestly, isn't it easy for us to miss the forest for the trees? How can we expect our flocks to believe if we ourselves are not believing Jesus and His Word? Without Jesus and His Word dwelling in our hearts, we will not overflow with Him and His Spirit. Our efforts will ring hollow. Paul puts it this way:

> If I speak in the tongues of men and
> of angels, but have not love, I am a noisy
> gong or a clanging cymbal.
>
> I CORINTHIANS 13:1

None of us wants to annoy others as a gong gone wrong. But without a personal heart connection to God's heart of love, we labor in our own strength. One of my leaders referred to this kind of fruit as being like the "fake grapes" found in her grandma's kitchen. Rather, we are after the juicy-sweet fruit of the Spirit that comes from abiding in the True Vine.

To overflow with Christ, one must first abide in Him:

> Abide in me, and I in you. As the branch
> cannot bear fruit by itself, unless it abides
> in the vine, neither can you, unless you
> abide in me.
>
> JOHN 15:4

Abiding in Jesus is the secret, powerful ingredient to leading Bible study. Okay, maybe it's not so secret, but it is powerful! Some days we feel that heart connection with God and other days we do not, but we can know we are abiding when we are obeying and seeking to follow His will. Fruit will follow.

Are you daily abiding with the Word from the inside out? Our character and our inner lives ought to align with our outward appearance. There is nothing more effective than a leader leading others with a humble and authentic heart. This transformation happens as a man or a woman applies Scripture, yields to God's will, and allows for the Spirit's holy work to happen within his or her own heart. That leads to true beauty. It's super attractive. Others will want to follow. Peter says it this way:

> Let your adorning be the hidden person of
> the heart with the imperishable
> beauty of a gentle and quiet spirit, which
> in God's sight is very precious.
>
> I PETER 3:4

GUARDING YOUR HEART WITH **PRAYER**

Here again, the need for prayer is obvious, but sometimes when we get caught up in the preparation details, we overlook the obvious. Pray, pray, and pray! If Jesus required prayer in order to remain in relationship and united with the Father in both purpose and mission, we surely require it more. Prayer helps us to stay focused on Christ and remember that He is the Good Shepherd who leads the way to green pastures and quiet waters. As we study His Word, we desire to follow Christ to these places that teem with His life and living water. However, without Christ to do the heavy lifting of paving the way and clearing the path, we will struggle to get there. And so, we pray.

Set aside time to pray for Bible study. Even before the Bible study semester begins, take one day away from other activities to commune with God and commit the weeks of study to Him.

Remember that prayer is simply sharing your heart and relating with God. It involves both speaking and listening. I find using the acronym **P.R.A.Y.** to be useful, especially when praying in groups. This template easily allows groups to walk through four steps of prayer:

P	PRAISE	Praise God for who He is.

Blessed be the God and Father of our Lord Jesus Christ!
1 Peter 1:3

Short "popcorn prayers" of praise like Peter's easily allow everyone to participate. Simple words and phrases to worship God work best:

I praise You, God, as the Light of the World.   Lord, You are Life.
I praise You for You are Mighty to Save.   You are Truth.

Beginning group sessions with praise turns our hearts toward God.

R	REPENT	Confess and agree with God concerning sin.

**If we confess our sins, he is faithful and just to forgive
us our sins and to cleanse us from all unrighteousness.**
1 John 1:9

Offer group members a silent moment to allow for private confession.

A	ADORE	Admire and thank God for His ways.

**Give thanks in all circumstances; for this is the will of
God in Christ Jesus for you.**
1 Thessalonians 5:18

Thanksgiving is a beautiful way to end a Bible study session. Together give thanks for all that God revealed.

Y	YIELD	Acknowledge your dependence on God. Yield to His ways.

**Humble yourselves, therefore, under the mighty hand of
God so that at the proper time he may exalt you, casting
all your anxieties on him, because he cares for you.**
1 Peter 5:6-7

With Peter's encouragement, give every concern to the Lord!

With that, what sorts of things shall we yield to God? Here are a few ideas and ways to align with God's heart:

- May God be glorified through the study.
- May women begin to hunger and thirst for God and His Word.
- May God's will be accomplished in the hearts of women.
- May women believe in Jesus and cast their worries to Him.
- May women's hearts be united with His and with one another.
- May God offer protection from all distractions as women study His Word.
- May God's Word transform hearts and lives, that women would begin to think and live differently.

GUARDING YOUR HEART WITH **THE WORD**

Read. Reflect. Remember His Word.

Whether teaching a large group or facilitating discussion in a small group, it's easy for leaders to fall into the trap of thinking that we need to have all of the right answers. Furthermore, we often feel the need to be able to speak all those answers eloquently. Due to this false thinking, many leaders spend countless hours scouring commentaries, and we wear ourselves out! After all, God's Word is so deep and rich that we will not plumb the depths of a Scripture passage in just one week. Thinking we need to have all the *right* answers is a fallacy.

Yes! Without a doubt, commentaries have their valuable place for solid interpretation. (Interpretation is that portion of inductive study where everyone should all be on the same page.) However, the risk for leaders who spend too much time delving into commentaries is that the workbook journal—as well as the teaching and discussion times—will reflect the commentaries rather than the Scripture itself.

To counter this, we simply need time in God's Word. As we read, observe, and marinate in the Bible text itself, God's Spirit teaches and leads. His Word speaks on its own. It's powerful and effective. We can trust in it!

> So shall my word be that goes out from
> my mouth; it shall not return to me empty,
> but it shall accomplish that which I
> purpose, and shall succeed in the thing
> for which I sent it.
>
> ISAIAH 55:11

Read, read, and read again. As mentioned in the introduction, read the Scripture passage using various translations. Read aloud and read slowly. Ponder. Listen to the Word while driving. Talk about what you are learning and discovering in the Word with family and friends. This will help you be prepared to speak about it when it is time for Bible study. Just as we marinate meat to soften, tenderize, and flavor it, we "sit in" the text, allowing God's Spirit to soften, tenderize, and flavor our hearts and minds with His personal message.

> I have stored up your word in my heart,
> that I might not sin against you.
>
> PSALM 119:11

A challenging, but brilliant way to soak in Scripture is memorization. Memorization is hard work, but the pay-off is great. Scripture becomes embedded within us and can overflow from the heart when needed. Certainly, those scriptures guard my own heart. And in leading, I have noticed that reciting Scripture over women deeply touches their hearts in a way that nothing else does. I highly recommend memorizing at least one key verse from the study.

Ideally, when studying in groups, teachers and small group leaders should prepare the study a week ahead of time. Yep! You read that right. Seek to be one week ahead of the regular study schedule. Then allow time for leaders to review together before leading and teaching in groups the following week. The benefits of discussing, sharing, and grappling with the Word as leaders is priceless for preparation and confidence in leading. Also, through that time, God will knit together the hearts of the leaders. That dynamic will then transform the ethos, or heart, of the group as a whole.

FRIENDS, MAY WE GUARD OUR HEARTS.

With Jesus, prayer and His Word, we are well-equipped to love and lead transformative conversations around our Bible study tables.

> But you will receive power when the **Holy Spirit** has come upon you, and you will be my witnesses in Jerusalem and in all Judea and Samaria, and to the end of the earth.
>
> ACTS 1:8

The following tools and resources included in this appendix may provide additional help and support as you endeavor to lead your group. Use them however you find them to be helpful.

- Effective Leadership Guide
- Weekly Preparation Guide
- Bible Study Schedule
- Small Group Roster
- Attendance Record
- Prayer Log

effective *leadership*

A GUIDE TO LEADING A SMALL GROUP EFFECTIVELY

Remember that the goal for our study is to see women growing in relationship with Christ and one another. You do not need to be a Bible expert to lead women in discussion about His Word. You only need a heart to love and encourage women. So, what does effective small group leadership look like?

ENCOURAGING | In an encouraging small group, all participants feel included and welcome to share freely. Thoughts and ideas are respected, and women are cheered on in their efforts to grow closer to God through their study of His Word.

BIBLICALLY SOUND | When we endeavor to create a biblically-sound environment, we point women in the direction of truth and correct doctrine, gently guiding them away from wrong thinking.

BALANCED | In a group that is balanced, shy or quiet women are drawn out and encouraged to participate in discussions, while "over-sharers" are encouraged to listen to others and not to dominate the conversation.

WISE | A wise small group leader recognizes when the conversation is getting off-topic or veering toward gossip. In such situations, it is a good idea to redirect women back to the ultimate focus of the meeting: God's Word.

PRAYERFUL | A prayerful group leader is an asset to her group. She prays regularly for her group members and facilitates opportunities for them to pray for one another.

CONFIDENTIAL | Group members should feel secure that the things they share will remain confidential. An effective small group leader is committed to preserving the privacy of her group members.

weekly preparation guide

PREPARING FOR SMALL-GROUP MEETINGS

WEEK 1: GENESIS 1

☐ Read the assigned daily passages.

☐ Use each daily framework to observe, interpret, and apply.

☐ Respond to all of the Day 5 questions.

☐ Pray for your small group meeting and for your group members.

1 What does this week's study tell me about God?	2 What does this week's study tell me about how I am to relate to Him?

WEEK 2: GENESIS 2

☐ Read the assigned daily passages.

☐ Use each daily framework to observe, interpret, and apply.

☐ Respond to all of the Day 5 questions.

☐ Pray for your small group meeting and for your group members.

1 What does this week's study tell me about God?	2 What does this week's study tell me about how I am to relate to Him?

WEEK 3: GENESIS 3

- ☐ Read the assigned daily passages.

- ☐ Use each daily framework to observe, interpret, and apply.

- ☐ Respond to all of the Day 5 questions.

- ☐ Pray for your small group meeting and for your group members.

1 What does this week's study tell me about God?	2 What does this week's study tell me about how I am to relate to Him?

WEEK 4: GENESIS 4 & 5

- ☐ Read the assigned daily passages.

- ☐ Use each daily framework to observe, interpret, and apply.

- ☐ Respond to all of the Day 5 questions.

- ☐ Pray for your small group meeting and for your group members.

1 What does this week's study tell me about God?	2 What does this week's study tell me about how I am to relate to Him?

WEEK 5: LUKE 1:1-38

☐ Read the assigned daily passages.

☐ Use each daily framework to observe, interpret, and apply.

☐ Respond to all of the Day 5 questions.

☐ Pray for your small group meeting and for your group members.

1 What does this week's study tell me about God?	2 What does this week's study tell me about how I am to relate to Him?

WEEK 6: LUKE 1:39-80

☐ Read the assigned daily passages.

☐ Use each daily framework to observe, interpret, and apply.

☐ Respond to all of the Day 5 questions.

☐ Pray for your small group meeting and for your group members.

1 What does this week's study tell me about God?	2 What does this week's study tell me about how I am to relate to Him?

WEEK 7: LUKE 2

☐ Read the assigned daily passages.

☐ Use each daily framework to observe, interpret, and apply.

☐ Respond to all of the Day 5 questions.

☐ Pray for your small group meeting and for your group members.

1 What does this week's study tell me about God?	2 What does this week's study tell me about how I am to relate to Him?

WEEK 8: OTHER PASSAGES WITH MARY

☐ Read the assigned daily passages.

☐ Use each daily framework to observe, interpret, and apply.

☐ Respond to all of the Day 5 questions.

☐ Pray for your small group meeting and for your group members.

1 What does this week's study tell me about God?	2 What does this week's study tell me about how I am to relate to Him?

WEEK 9: FINAL THOUGHTS | WRAPPING UP

☐ Respond to all of the Wrap-up questions

☐ Pray for your small group meeting and for your group members.

1 What does this week's study tell me about God?	2 What does this week's study tell me about how I am to relate to Him?

bible study *schedule*

EVE & MARY | A **SIMPLY BIBLE** STUDY

	READING ASSIGNMENT	SMALL GROUP MEETING DATE	LEADER MEETING DATE
WEEK 1			
WEEK 2			
WEEK 3			
WEEK 4			
WEEK 5			
WEEK 6			
WEEK 7			
WEEK 8			
WEEK 9			

I AM THE VINE; YOU ARE
THE BRANCHES. WHOEVER
ABIDES IN ME AND I IN HIM,
HE IT IS THAT BEARS MUCH
FRUIT, FOR APART FROM ME
YOU CAN DO NOTHING.

JOHN 15:5

small group *roster*

EVE & MARY | A **SIMPLY BIBLE** STUDY

PARTICIPANT LIST

1
2
3
4
5
6
7
8
9
10
11
12
13
14
15

NAME	
BIRTHDAY	
PHONE NUMBER	
EMAIL ADDRESS	
CONTACT METHOD	
NOTES	

NAME	
BIRTHDAY	
PHONE NUMBER	
EMAIL ADDRESS	
CONTACT METHOD	
NOTES	

NAME	
BIRTHDAY	
PHONE NUMBER	
EMAIL ADDRESS	
CONTACT METHOD	
NOTES	

NAME

BIRTHDAY	
PHONE NUMBER	
EMAIL ADDRESS	
CONTACT METHOD	

NOTES

NAME

BIRTHDAY	
PHONE NUMBER	
EMAIL ADDRESS	
CONTACT METHOD	

NOTES

NAME

BIRTHDAY	
PHONE NUMBER	
EMAIL ADDRESS	
CONTACT METHOD	

NOTES

NAME

BIRTHDAY	
PHONE NUMBER	
EMAIL ADDRESS	
CONTACT METHOD	

NOTES

NAME

BIRTHDAY	
PHONE NUMBER	
EMAIL ADDRESS	
CONTACT METHOD	

NOTES

NAME

BIRTHDAY	
PHONE NUMBER	
EMAIL ADDRESS	
CONTACT METHOD	

NOTES

NAME

BIRTHDAY

PHONE NUMBER

EMAIL ADDRESS

CONTACT METHOD

NOTES

NAME

BIRTHDAY

PHONE NUMBER

EMAIL ADDRESS

CONTACT METHOD

NOTES

NAME

BIRTHDAY

PHONE NUMBER

EMAIL ADDRESS

CONTACT METHOD

NOTES

NAME

BIRTHDAY	
PHONE NUMBER	
EMAIL ADDRESS	
CONTACT METHOD	

NOTES

NAME

BIRTHDAY	
PHONE NUMBER	
EMAIL ADDRESS	
CONTACT METHOD	

NOTES

NAME

BIRTHDAY	
PHONE NUMBER	
EMAIL ADDRESS	
CONTACT METHOD	

NOTES

attendance log

EVE & MARY | A **SIMPLY BIBLE** STUDY

PARTICIPANT'S NAME	WEEK 1	WEEK 2	WEEK 3	WEEK 4	WEEK 5
1					
2					
3					
4					
5					
6					
7					
8					
9					
10					
11					
12					
13					
14					
15					

attendance log

EVE & MARY | A **SIMPLY BIBLE** STUDY

	WEEK 6	WEEK 7	WEEK 8	WEEK 9

prayer log

EVE & MARY | A **SIMPLY BIBLE** STUDY

DATE	NAME	REQUEST	FOLLOW-UP

prayer log

DATE	NAME	REQUEST	FOLLOW-UP

prayer log

EVE & MARY | A **SIMPLY BIBLE** STUDY

DATE	NAME	REQUEST	FOLLOW-UP

prayer log

EVE & MARY | A **SIMPLY BIBLE** STUDY

DATE	NAME	REQUEST	FOLLOW-UP

prayer log

DATE	NAME	REQUEST	FOLLOW-UP

prayer log

EVE & MARY | A **SIMPLY BIBLE** STUDY

DATE	NAME	REQUEST	FOLLOW-UP

prayer log

EVE & MARY | A **SIMPLY BIBLE** STUDY

DATE	NAME	REQUEST	FOLLOW-UP

prayer log

EVE & MARY | A **SIMPLY BIBLE** STUDY

DATE	NAME	REQUEST	FOLLOW-UP

AND WE KNOW THAT
FOR THOSE WHO LOVE GOD
ALL THINGS WORK TOGETHER
FOR GOOD, FOR THOSE WHO
ARE CALLED ACCORDING
TO HIS PURPOSE.

ROMANS 8:28